Pimbley's
Dictionary of Heraldry

TOGETHER WITH AN

ILLUSTRATED SUPPLEMENT

By
ARTHUR FRANCIS PIMBLEY

BALTIMORE:
PUBLISHED BY THE AUTHOR
1908

PREFACE.

Armorial bearings, at first personal and afterward becoming hereditary, were supposed to have lost their usefulness with the fading of the age of chivalry. Their real use and importance, it is true, died with the passing of the armor-incased knight; nevertheless, heraldry remains a live institution, and will so continue as long as civilization and refinement last. If any doubt is felt of its vitality, we have but to view the evidence of it in the New World. For instance, the design of our national emblem, the Stars and Stripes, is taken from the arms of the immortal George Washington, who bore "Argent, two bar gules, in chief three mullets of the second." The arms of the State of Maryland are those of the Calverts, Barons of Baltimore and sometime Lords Proprietary of the Province of Maryland. Other States have adopted armorial bearings peculiar to their location or resources, such as the Indian and cactus of Florida, the badger of Wisconsin, the wheat field of Iowa and the mining implements of Colorado. In America also we have a large number of genealogical and hereditary societies. There is likewise a wide and general desire on the part of Americans to trace their pedigrees to their Old World ancestors, and to assume the arms belonging to them.

This ever-increasing interest in heraldry in the New World, as well as the scarcity of modern works on subjects heraldric, have induced the author to publish a work containing all the words, phrases, terms and tinctures belonging to the study of heraldry, together with a proper division or classification of arms, rules of blazonry, illustrations of the principal armorial bearings, different forms of the shield, etc.

THE AUTHOR.

PREFATORY NOTES.

In the DICTIONARY OF HERALDRY the definitions are given as briefly as possible consistent with their completeness, and set forth in as plain and simple form as the subject will permit, technical terms being done away with so far as practicable, and few abbreviations being used.

The author has attempted to trace the etymological history of each word, and when this proved futile the form of orthography adopted has been that recognized by the College of Arms.

It has been said by some writers that "there is no standard of pronunciation." The highest authority is the one in vogue, and the author has adopted the current pronunciation for the standard.

In the case of compound words, they will be found under the first element of the compound. For example, *Arms of Adoption* will be found under Arms; *counter-vair* under Counter, instead of after Counterpointe.

A word described as French does not mean merely that it is from the French. As a matter of fact, nearly every word in heraldry is French or of French origin. A French word, however, having an equivalent in English is marked thus: [French]. For example, Démembré in English blazonry would be Dismembered.

ABBREVIATIONS.

Arg.—Argent.

Az.—Azure.

Bart., Bt.—Baronet.

C. B.—Companion of the Bath.

C. D. S. O.—Companion of the Distinguished Service Order.

Chap.—Chapter.

C. I.—Order of the Crown of India.

C. I. E.—Companion of the Order of the Indian Empire.

C. M. G.—Companion of the Order of St. Michael and St. George.

C. R.—Keeper of the Rolls.

C. S.—Clerk of the Signet.

C. S. I.—Companion of the Star of India.

Er.—Ermine.

G. C. B.—Grand Cross of the Bath.

G. C. H.—Grand Cross of the Guelphs of Hanover.

G. C. L. H.—Grand Cross of the Legion of Honor.

G. C. M. G.—Grand Cross of St. Michael and St. George.

G. C. S. I.—Grand Commander of the Star of India.

Gu.—Gules.

H. C.—Heralds' College.

Her.—Heraldry, heraldic.

K. B.—Knight of the Bath.

K. C. B.—Knight Commander of the Bath.

K. C. H.—Knight Commander of the Guelphs of Hanover.

K. C. M. G.—Knight Commander of St. Michael and St. George.

K. C. S.—Knight of the Order of Charles III of Spain.

K. C. S. I.—Knight Commander of the Star of India.

K. G.—Knight of the Garter.

K. G. C.—Knight Grand Cross.

K. G. C. B.—Knight Grand Cross of the Bath.

K. G. F.—Knight of the Golden Fleece.

K. G. H.—Knight of the Guelphs of Hanover.

K. L. B.—Knight of Leopold of Belgium.

K. L. H.—Knight of the Legion of Honor.

K. M.—Knight of Malta.

Kn. N. S.—Knight of the Loyal Northern Star (Sweden).

Knt., Kn t.—Knight.

K. P.—Knight of St. Patrick.

K. S.—Knight of the Sword (Sweden).

K. T.—Knight of the Thistle.

K. T. S.—Knight of the Tower and Sword (Portugal).

L. C. B.—Lord Chief Baron.

Ld.—Lord.

Ldp.—Lordship.

M. H.—Most Honorable.

Ppr.—Proper.

P. S.—Privy Seal.

Pt.—Potent.

Pur.—Purpure.

Rt. Hon.—Right Honorable.

Sa.—Sable.

U. K. A.—Ulster King-at-Arms.

V. C.—Victoria Cross.

Vis.—Viscount.

V. R.—Queen Victoria. (Latin, *Victoria Regina.*)

Vr.—Vair.

Vt.—Vert.

A DICTIONARY
OF
ʻHERALDRY.

A.

Abased—This term is used (1) when the wings, for instance, instead of being expanded, with their apices pointing outward, either look down toward the point of the shield, or else are shut; (2) when a chevron, fesse or another ordinary is borne lower than its usual situation.

WINGS ABASED.

Abasement—[See ABASED.]

Abatelement—(Ab-a-te′-le-mang) A mark of disgrace affixed to an escutcheon. [See ABATEMENT.]

Abatement—Abatements are real or imaginary marks of disgrace affixed to an escutcheon on account of some flagrantly dishonorable action on the part of the bearer. There is scarcely an instance on record, however, of such marks of disgrace having been actually affixed to an escutcheon. (Sometimes called rebatements.)

Abyss—The center of an escutcheon. For example, to bear a fleur-de-lis in abyss is to have it placed in the middle of the shield free from any other bearing.

Abyssal—Pertaining to an abyss.

Accident—(Ac′-ci-dent) An additional mark on a coat of arms, which may be retained or eliminated without altering its essential character.

Accolade—(Ac′-co lade) The ceremony by which in mediæval times one was dubbed a knight. Antiquaries are not agreed on what this was. It has been made an embrace around the neck, a kiss or a slight blow upon the cheek or shoulder.
"The new attorney-general having stooped down without objection to the usual accolade."—*Townsend's Lives of 12 Eminent Judges: Lord Eldon.*

Accolle—(Ac-col′-le) Gorged or collared. as lions, dogs and other animals sometimes are in escutcheons.
Wreathed, entwined or joined together, as two shields sometimes are by their sides. The arms of a husband and wife were often thus placed. *(Gloss. of Heraldry, 1847.)*

Used substantively: (1) An animal with a crown on its head or a collar around its neck; (2) two shields united to each other by their sides; (3) a key, baton, mace, sword or other implement or weapon placed saltirewise behind the shield. *(Ibid.)*

Accompanied — (Ac-com'-pan-ied) Between. For example, accompanied by four crescents, would mean between four crescents.

Accompaniment — (Ac-com'-pan-i-ment) Any additions made to a shield by way of ornament, as supporters, etc.

Accost—[See ACCOSTED.]

Accosted — (Ac-cost'-ed) Applied to a charge supported on both sides by other charges. Example: A pale accosted by six mullets. This term is also applied to two animals proceeding side by side.

Accoutre—(Ak-ku'-ter) To dub a knight.
"One was accoutred when the cry began,
Knight of the Silver Moon, Sir Marmadan,
His vow was (and he will perform his vow),
Armed at all points, with terror on his brow,
To judge the land, to purge atrocious crimes."
Cowper: Anti-Thelyphthora.

Achievement—(A-chieve'-ment) A complete heraldic composition, showing a shield with its quarterings, impalements, supporters, crest, motto, etc. This term is applied especially to a funeral escutcheon, exhibiting the rank and family of a deceased nobleman or gentleman, which at his death is placed in front of his house or in some other prominent place. [This is commonly called HATCHMENT.]

Acorned—(A'korned) An oak with acorns on it. (Placed on an escutcheon.)

Addition—Something added to a coat of arms as a mark of honor, such as, for instance, a bordure, a quarter, a canton, a gyron or a pile. [Opposed to ABATEMENT.]
"They clepe us drunkards, and with swinish phrase
Soil our addition; and indeed it takes
From our achievements."
—*Shakespeare: Hamlet, 1, 4.*

Addorse—(Ad-dor'se) To place back to back.

Addorsed—(Ad-dor'st) *Used as an adjective:* Two animals on a coat of arms set or turned back to back. This term is occasionally used for other figures capable of being placed back to back.

ADDORSED.

Adosse—The French word sometimes used for ADDORSED.

Adoption—*Arms of Adoption.* [See under ARMS.]

Adoptive—Adoptive arms are those held by a person not by right of descent or in virtue of himself, but merely by the gift or consent of another.

Adorned — (Ad-orn'ed) Ornamented or furnished with a charge.

Adumbration—(Ad-um-bra'-tion) A figure on a coat of arms traced in outline only, or painted in a darker shade of the same color as the field on which it is represented. Families who had lost their estates, but not their armorial bearings, are said to have occasionally adopted this method of indicating their peculiar position. (Also called *transparency.*)

Affrontee—(Af-fron'-ta) Two animals on

AFFRONTEE.

a coat of arms facing each other.

Face to face, as contradistinguished from back to back. [See ADDORSED.]

Confronting one another is a phrase sometimes used in this connection.

Agacella—(Ag-a-cel'la) An antelope, or a tiger with-horns and hoofs.

Aiguisce—(Ag-wis-se') Sharply pointed. Applied especially to a cross on an escutcheon which has its four angles sharpened, but still terminating in obtuse angles. It differs from the cross *fitchee* in that whereas the latter tapers by degrees to a point, the former does so only at the ends.

Ailettes—(Ai'-lettes) Small escutcheons fastened to the shoulders of armed knights. (Sometimes called *emerasses*.) They were of steel; were introduced in the reign of Edward I, and were the ancestor of the modern epaulet.

Aisle—(I-la) Winged.

Alaund—A dog. Specifically, a hunting dog.

Albany—One of the herald's of the Lord Lyon's Court. Scotland.

Alberia—(Al-ber'-i-a) A plain shield; without ornament or armorial bearings.

Allerion—(Al-ler'-i-on) An eagle without beak or feet, and with wings expanded, their points turned downward. (Denoting imperialists vanquished and disarmed.)

ALLERION.

Alliance—*Arms of alliance.* [See under ARMS.

Allocamelus—(Al-lo-ca-mel'-us) The ass-camel, a mythical animal compounded of the camel and the ass. This was used as a crest by the Eastland Company.

Allumee—(Al-lu'-may') This term is used to describe the eyes of animals when they are depicted sparkling or red.

Allusive—*Allusive Arms.* [See under ARMS.]

Alternate—*Alternate quarters:* A term applied to the first and fourth quarters on an escutcheon, which are generally of the same kind. Also applied to the second and fourth, which also similarly resemble each other.

Ambulant—This signifies walking; co-ambulant, walking together.

Amethyst—(Am'-eth-yst) The term applied to the color called purpure when describing the armorial bearings of peers.

Amphisien cockatrice— (Am-phis'i-en cock'-a-trice) A name for the mythical animal called the Basilisk. It resembles a cockatrice, but is two-headed, the second head being affixed to its tail.

Anchor—In heraldry the anchor is an emblem of hope.

Anchored Cross—In this cross the four extremities resemble the flukes of an anchor. It is also called *anchry or anore.* It is emblematic of hope through the cross of Christ.

ANCHORED CROSS.

"Which hope we have as an anchor of the soul, both sure and steadfast,"—*Heb. iv, 19.*

Ancient (Anshent)—The guidon used at funerals. A small flag ending in a point.

Anime—(An-e-may') Of a different tincture from the animal itself. The term is used when wild animals are represented with fire proceeding from their mouths. Also called *incensed*.

Annodated—(An'-no-dated) Bowed, embowed or bent like the letter S.

Annulate—(An'-u-lat) Having a ring or annulet. (Used specifically of a cross with its extremities thus fretted.)

Annulet—(An'-u-let) A ring borne on an escutcheon. Originally it stood as the symbol of nobility and jurisdiction, being the gage of royal favor and protection. In describing arms the color of the annulet should always be expressed.

¶ When used as a difference, the annulet represents the fifth son.

ANNULET.

Anserated Cross—(An'-ser-a-ted) A cross with one of its extremities shaped like the heads of lions, eagles, etc.

Ante—(An'-tay') Engrafted or joined into each other in any way, as by dovetails, swallowtails or rounds.

Antelope—*Agacella* is the heraldic antelope. Brooke, Lord Cobham, had for a dexter supporter an agacella, horned, tusked and armed or.

Apaume—(A-pa'u-mé) Appalmed. A hand opened so as to exhibit the palm.

A baronet of England or Ireland bears a sinister hand couped gules on an inescutcheon or a canton. It is blazoned "argent, a sinister hand, couped at the wrist, and *apaume*, gules."

Apple of Grenada—The pomegranate.

Appointee—(Ap-poi'n-tay) Pointed. Applied to things which touch at the points or ends, as two swords touching each other at their points or tips.

Aquilate—(Ak'-wil-ate) To adorn with eagles' heads.

Aquilated—(Ak'-wil-ated) Adorned with eagles' heads. (Used almost exclusively in the past participle.)

Arbalest—[See ARBLAST.]

Arblast—A crossbow, consisting of a steel bow set in a shaft of wood and furnished with a string and trigger. It was not a poular weapon, as it required no strength or manliness in its use. (Also written arbalist, arbalest and arbalet.)

Arched—Signifies that an ordinary on an escutcheon is bent or bowed. (Sometimes called *Archy.)

Archy—[See ARCHED.]

Argent—(Ar'-jent) White. The silvery color on coats of arms. In the arms of princes it is sometimes called *lune*, and in those of peers *pearl*. In engravings it is generally represented by the natural color of the paper. It represents purity, innocence, beauty or gentleness.

"He beareth gules upon his shield,
A chevron argent in the field."
—*Tales of a Wayside Inn.*

ARGENT.

Used as an adjective: Of the coloring of coats armor.

"Rinaldo flings
As swift as fiery lightning kindled new;
His argent eagle with her silver wings,
In field of azure, fair Erminia knew."
—*Fairfax.*

Arm—The human arm is sometimes used in emblazoning. Tremaine of Colacombe bore gules, three dexter arms conjoined at the shoulder, flexed in triangle or, fisted argent.

The arm is often found as part of the crest. [See CUBIT ARM.]

Armed—(1) Furnished with arms. (2) Adding to anything that which will give it greater strength or efficiency. (3) The term *armed of* applies to a beast of prey when his teeth and claws are differently colored from the rest of his body. It applies also to predatory birds when their talons and beaks are differently colored from the rest of the body.

(4) *Armed at all points*, in days gone by, meant a man covered with armor except his face.

Armor—*Coat Armor.* [The same as COAT OF ARMS.]

Armor Buckle—A lozenge-shaped buckle.

Armorial—(Ar-mo'ri-al). *As an adjective:* Pertaining or relating to heraldic arms.

As substantive: A book containing coats of arms. Thus the phrase occurs, "the French armorial," "the Spanish armorial," etc.

Armorist—One well acquainted with coats of arms; skilled in heraldry. *(Bailey.)*

Armory—From the word *armor*, appertaining to coats of arms.

Arms—*Arms* or *Armories* were so called because originally displayed upon defensive arms, and *coats of arms* because formerly embroidered upon the surcoat or camis worn over the armor. The term coat of arms, once introduced, was afterward retained, even when displayed elsewhere than on the coat. In the days when knights were so encased in armor that no means of identifying them was left, the practice was introduced of painting their insignia of honor on their shield as an easy method of distinguishing them. Originally these were granted only to individuals, but were afterward made hereditary by King Richard I, during his crusade to Palestine. They may be divided into two general classes: (1) *Public*, as those of kingdoms, provinces, bishoprics, corporate bodies, etc., and (2) *private*, being those of private families. These two classes are again separated into many subdivisions, founded mainly on the different methods by which they were granted.

ARMS OF ADOPTION—This term is used in a case where the last representative of an aristocratic family adopts an outsider to assume his armorial bearings and inherit his estates.

ARMS OF ALLIANCE—Arms which came into a man's possession by matrimonial alliances, as the arms of his wife which are impaled with his own, and those of heiresses, which he in like manner quarters. To illustrate: When Gilbert Talbot (who died in 1274) married Gwenllian, heiress of the Welsh Prince Rhys ap Griffith, he laid aside his paternal coat—"bendy of 10 pieces, agent and gules"—and adopted that of the lady— "gules, a lion rampant or, within a border engrailed of the field"—as still used by the Earls of Shrewsbury.

ARMS OF ASSUMPTION—Those arms which a person may legitimately assume.

ARMS OF ATTRIBUTION—Arms that are fictitious, such as indulged in to an absurd extent by the heralds of the fifteenth and sixteenth centuries.

"Almost all the older genealogists attribute coats of arms to ancestors long before they were in use. On the tomb of Queen Elizabeth are emblazoned the arms of William the Conqueror and Matilda of Flanders, and of Henry I and Matilda of Scotland, all, of course, pure inventions. It is only of very late years, since a critical spirit has found its way even into heraldry, that these absurdities have been exposed."— *Ency. Brit., vol. xi (1902).*

ARMS OF COMMUNITY—Those borne by corporations, religious houses, colleges, cities and boroughs, inns of court, guilds and the cinque ports, some of which go back to an early period.

ARMS OF CONCESSION—Arms granted by a sovereign to commemorate some great deed. The heart on the arms of the Douglases is in memory of the mission of James Lord Douglas with the heart of Robert Bruce to the Holy Land. The families of De la Warr, Pelham, Vane and Fane bear arms in allusion to the share their ancestors had in the capture of John of France at Poitiers.

ARMS OF DOMINION—Are those belonging to empires, kingdoms, principalities, states, etc., officially used by the ruler *de facto*. The origin of some of these arms is obscure, such as the three legs conjoined in triangle of the Isle of Man and the lion of Scotland. Occasionally the arms of dominion were those of an early sovereign or governor. Thus the lions of England belonged to the Plantagnet kings. In the United States the Stars and Stripes, now so well known throughout the world, had their origin in the coat of arms of the first President, the immortal George Washington, whose English ancestors bore "argent, two bars gules, in chief three mullets of the second." The arms of the State of Maryland are those borne by Cecillius Calvert, second Lord Baltimore, Lord Proprietary of the colony.

ARMS OF FAMILY—Those received by some distinguished person and borne with modifications by all his descendants.

ARMS OF HONOR—The same as *Arms of Concession*.

ARMS OF OFFICE—Those borne by holders of certain offices which designate that office. For instance, the ancestors of the Dukes of Ormond, being hereditary butlers of Ireland, bore three covered cups. Garter, the principal king-at-arms of England, bears "argent, a cross gules, on a chief azure a crown or, encircled with a garter of the order buckled and nowed between a lion of England and a lily of France."

ARMS OF PATRONAGE—(1) Arms borne by the lesser gentry which were derived from the arms of the greater; arms on which there is some mark of subjection or dependence. (2) Arms to indicate the connection between the follower and his feudal lord. (3) Arms added to the family arms as a token of superiority, right or jurisdiction.

ARMS OF PRETENSION—Arms quartered by a sovereign belonging to a state over which he does not hold authority. Nearly all the earlier European sovereigns bore arms of this character. The kings of England, from Edward III until 1801, in the reign of George III, bore the lilies of France. The treaty of Amiens (January 1, 1801) stipulated that this quartering of the French arms should be abandoned.

ARMS OF SUCCESSION—The same as *Feudal Arms*.

ARMS ROYAL—The personal arms borne by the sovereign of a country, as distinguished from those borne by him in his official capacity, being those of the country over which he rules. As set forth in *Arms of Dominion*, the personal arms of a ruler sometimes become those of the country. On the other hand, neither the arms of Baliol, Bruce nor Stuart ever became the arms of Scotland. Cromwell placed his arms on an escutcheon of pretense over those of the commonwealth, and William of Nassau did the same with those of England.

ALLUSIVE ARMS—(Called also *canting* or *punning* arms, and by the French *Armes parlantes*) are those in which the charges suggest the bearer's name. Thus were the castle and lion for Castile and Leon, the fers de cheval of Ferrers, the corbeau or raven for Corbet, the herons of Heron, the falcon of Falconer, the swine's head of Swinbourne, the hammers of Hammerton and the swallows (hirondelles) of Arundel. Allusive arms were treated with respect until the time of James I, when they fell into disrepute.

ASSUMPTIVE ARMS—This now applies to arms which have been appropriated without proper authority. Originally, however, the term had a different meaning, as see the following:

"* * * Assumptive arms are such as a person has a title to bear, by virtue of some action done or performed by him, which by birth he could not wear; as if a person that has naturally no coat should, in lawful war, take a prince or nobleman prisoner, he has from that time a right to bear the arms of such prisoner by virtue of that military law that the dominion of things taken in lawful war passes to the conqueror."—*Dych: Dict. (1758).*

CANTING ARMS—The same as *Allusive Arms*.

FEUDAL ARMS—The arms borne by the possessors of certain lordships or estates.

PATERNAL ARMS—Those that descend by custom to the male heir. The descendants of females (heiresses) can only quarter their arms, except by special license.

Arriswise—(Ar'-ris-wise) With one angle facing; showing the top and two sides. Said of a rectangular bearing, such as an altar.

Arrondee—(Ar-ron'-dy) Made round.

Arrondell—A swallow.

Arrow—The arrow is frequently displayed in heraldry, either singly or in sheaves.

Ashen Keys—The seed vessels of the ash tree. Occasionally represented on an escutcheon.

ASHEN KEYS.

Aspect—The position which an animal occupies with regard to the eye of the spectator. It may be (1) *full aspect*, that is, full-faced, looking toward the spectator; (2) *passant*, with its side toward him; (3) *trian aspect*, neither the one or the other, but between the two.

Aspectant—(As-pect'-ant) A term applied to two birds facing each other, or looking at each other.

Aspecting—[The same as ASPECTANT.]

Aspersed—(As-per'sed) Strewn or powdered with a number of small charges. [See SEME.]

Assaultant — (As-sa'ult-ant) Assailant. Applied to a predatory animal when represented on the escutcheon as if leaping on its prey.

Assumption—*Arms of Assumption.* [See under ARMS.]

Assumptive—*Assumptive Arms.* [See under ARMS.]

Assurgent—(As-sur'-gent) Rising out of.

At Gaze—Applied to the hart, buck, stag or hind when represented full-faced, or with the face directly to the front.

Athole—One of the pursuivants of the Office of Arms, Ireland.

Attire—(At-ti're) The single horn of a stag. (The plural *attires* is used for two horns.)

Attired—Ornamented with horns or antlers. Applied to the stag or hart. A reindeer is represented with *double attires*—one pair erect and the other drooping. *(Boutell: English Heraldry.)*

   "Attired is a term used among heralds when they have occasion to speak of the horns of a buck or stag."—*Bullokar: Eng. Expos. (1656).*

ATTIRED.

Attribution—*Arms of Attribution.* [See under ARMS.]

Augmentation—*Arms of Augmentation of Honor*—A grant from a sovereign of an additional charge on a coat of arms to commemorate some great deed or a notable event. [See *Arms of Concession*, under ARMS.]

Aulned—(awn'd) Awned; bearded (Used of ears of corn.)

Au vol—[French.] On the wing. (Said of a bird. [VOLANT.]

Avellane Cross—(A-vel'-lane) A cross

resembling four filberts.

AVELLANE CROSS.

Averdant—(A-ver'-dant) Covered with green herbage. The term is used specially of a mount in base. *(Gloss. of Heraldry.)*

Averlye—(Av'-ar-lie) The same as AS-PERSED, which see.

Aversant—(A-ver'-sant) Turned away. Applied to a hand of which only the back can be seen. Sometimes called *dorsed*.

Awned—[See AULNED.]

Axe—[See BATTLE AXE.]

Aylet—(Ay'-let) A name used to designate the Cornish chough *(Fregilus graculus)*, a bird belonging to the crow family.

Ayrant—[See EYRANT.]

Azure—Bright blue. Used especially in describing the escutcheons of gentlemen beneath the degree of baron. The same color on a nobleman's coat is called sapphire, from the stone, and that on the coat of a sovereign prince Jupiter, from the planet of that name. Engravers represent azure in heraldry by horizontal lines.

B.

Bachelor—A member of the oldest, but now the lowest, order of knighthood in Great Britain.

Formerly a Bachelor meant a knight without a sufficient number of vassals to have his banner carried before him in battle.

Badge—A distinctive mark; a cognizance. It is somewhat similar to a crest, but was not placed on a wreath, nor was it worn on the helmet. The badge was a possession of princes, noblemen and other gentlemen of rank, and to this day is retained by some of those houses. The badge *Badge of the Prince of Wales* of the Plantagenets was the broom plant *(Planta genista);* the line of Lancaster had a red rose, while the badge of the house of York was a white rose.

In former times badges were embroidered on the sleeves of the servants and retainers, and the practice is still in use to some extent.

In the time of Henry IV the terms *livery* and *badge* seem to have been synonymous.

Badger—(Bad'-ger) A mammalian animal found in England and on the Continent. It is often used in heraldry. It is sometimes called a gray and also a brock.

Bagwin—(Bag'-win) A mythical animal, having the tail of a horse, and with long horns curved over the ears.

Balls—Balls, occasionally tasselled, are sometimes shown on charges.

Ballet—(Bal'-lay) A bearing which consists of bezants, plates, hurts, etc., distinguished from each other by their color.

Bande—(Ban'-dy) The French word for the term *in bend.*

Banded—(Band'-ed) When a garb is bound together with a band of a different tincture it is described as *banded of* that tincture.

Bandrol—(Band'-rol) A small streamer depending from the crook of a crozier and folding over the staff. *(Universal Dict.)*

The small silk flag which occasionally hangs from a trumpet. *(Johnson.)*

Banner—A square flag, generally embroidered with the owner's arms. No one below the rank of knight banneret is entitled to a banner.

Banneret—*Knight Banneret.* The institution is an ancient one, and its members, who had the privilege of leading their retainers in battle under their own flag, ranked next in order below the Knights of the Garter, provided they were created on the battle field by the King; otherwise they took rank after baronets. The order is now extinct.

Bar—An ordinary which crosses the shield horizontally. It differs from a fesse in that it occupies only one-fifth of the field. There is room for but four bars on a shield.

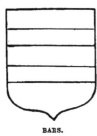

BARS.

BARS GEMEL—Bars placed parallel to each other. A bar with closets placed in couples.

IN BAR—Charges arranged in two or more rows. It differs from *in fesse* in that the latter term signifies charges in a single row.

Barbed—Bearded. Used specifically of the arrow; also, of the five leaflets in the compound leaf of some roses.

Barbel—(Bar'-bel) A "bearded' fish found abundantly in the Thames and Lea. It is an early heraldic bearing.

Barded—A horse in harness is said to be barded and caparisoned. Originally a barded horse was one protected by metal trappings, such as those ridden by knights in mediæval times. The armor covered the neck, breast and shoulders.

Barnacle—An instrument for pinching a horse's nose for the purpose of restraining him.

Baron—A nobleman of the lowest order of the English peerage.

BARONESS—The wife of a baron, or a woman who holds the baronial dignity in her own right.

BARON AND FEME—Applied when the coats of arms of a man and his wife are borne *per pale* in the same escutcheon. When the wife is not an heiress her arms occupy the sinister side, and the husband's the dexter. If she is an heiress, the husband bears her arms on an escutcheon of pretense.

Baronet—The lowest British titled order that is hereditary. They are supposed to take precedence immediately after the barons, but in reality their rank is inferior to that of the Knights of the Garter. . The badge of a baronet is, sinister, a hand gules ("a bloody hand") in a field argent.

Barred—Supplied with bars; placed between bars. [BAR.] [BARRY.]

Barring—The same as BARRY or BARRULY. (*Chaucer.*)

Barrulet—(Bar'-rul-et) The barrulet is one-fourth of a bar, and occupies a twentieth part of the field; never borne singly. Sometimes called a *bracelet*. When used in couples barrulets are *bars gemel*.

Barrully—[The same as BARRY.]

Barry—(Bar'-ry) The division of the field by horizontal lines into a certain number of equal parts.

BARRY BENDY—Signifies a field divided barwise and bendwise, the tinctures being counterchanged.

BARRY BENDY.

BARRY BENDY SINISTER—A combination of barry and bendy sinister.

BARRY BENDY DEXTER AND SINISTER—

A combination of barry and bendy dexter and sinister. (Sometimes called *barry lozengy*.)

BARRY LOZENGY—The same as *barry pily*.

BARRY PILY—Divided into an equal number of pieces by piles placed horizontally across the shield.

Bars gemel—(jem'-el) Two horizontal bars on a field close to each other ; a pair of bars.

BARS GEMEL.

Barwise—Arranged horizontally in two or more rows.

Base—The lower part of a shield. Specifically, the width of a bar parted off from the lower part of the shield by a line horizontally drawn. (Sometimes called *base-bar*, *baste* and *plain point.)*

Base-bar—[See BASE.]

Basilisk—(Bas'-i-lisk) A fabulous animal which was believed to be so deadly that even its breath was fatal to those who came near it. It somewhat resembled the Cockatrice, differing, however, in that it had two heads, the second being at the extremity of its tail. This additional head is the cause of it sometimes being called AMPHISIEN COCKATRICE.

Basket—A winnowing basket.

Baston—[See BATON.]

Bat—The Bat figures to some extent in heraldry, often called a reremouse.

Bath—*Order of the Bath.* An English order of knighthood, which was instituted by Henry IV in 1399, and revived by George I in 1725. It derives its name from the fact that candidates for initiation were required to bathe the night before investiture.

Baton—(Bat'-on) The Baton, or, more fully, the Baton Sinister, is a diminutive of the bend sinister, of which it is one-fourth the width. It is a rare bearing, and generally denotes illegitimacy. Sometimes, though erroneously, called a fissure.

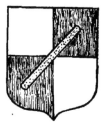

BATON SINISTER.

Battering-ram—A bearing representing the engine used in ancient times to beat down the walls of besieged places. It was a large beam, with a head of iron, sometimes made to resemble the head of a ram. The battering-ram is borne by the Earls of Lindsey.

Battle-axe—A weapon like an axe, formerly used in battle, hence it became conspicuous in heraldry.

Battled—(Bat'-tled) A chief, chevron, fesse, etc., borne on one side in the form of the battlements of a castle.

Battled-embattled—[See GRADY.]

Bayard—A bay horse.

Beaked—When the beak and legs of a bird are of a different tincture from the body it is said to be beaked and membered of that tincture.

Bear—The bear is one of the beasts of heraldry. Early examples are the arms of Beresford and of Fitz Urse.

Bearer—The supporter of a shield on an escutcheon.

Bearing—A charge; any single charge or emblem included within an escutcheon. (Generally used in the plural, as "armorial bearings.")

Beauseant—(Bo'-ze-aunt) The banner borne by the Knights Templar in the thirteenth century. It was of cloth, sable and argent.

Bebally—A word used by some of the old writers for party per pale. *(Parker: Gloss. of Her.)*

Becque—[See BECQUE.]

Bee—Sometimes made use of in heraldry. Sir Robert Peel used bees in his arms, and so did Sir Richard Arkwright.

Belic—(Bel'-ic) A term sometimes used for gules. *(Universal Dict.)*

Bell—Church bells have been made use of in heraldry, though not frequently. The same can be said of hawks' bells.

Belled—When a falcon or a hawk has bells affixed to its legs it is said to be *belled.*

Belt—A badge of knighthood.

Bend—One of the ordinaries. It is formed of two lines, and is drawn from the dexter chief to the sinister base point of the escutcheon. It generally occupies one-fifth of the field; but formerly it was one-fifth only when plain, and one-third when charged.

BEND.

The bend is said to have been derived from the border on a woman's cap known as a *bend.* It is possible that its origin was a representation of the baldric. According to some, the origin was a scaling ladder. In the beginning of heraldry the bend was a mark of cadency, but later became an honorable ordinary.

"The diminutives of the bend are the bendlet, garter or gartier, which is half its width; the cost or cottice, which is one-fourth; and the riband, which is one-eighth."—*Gloss. of Her.*

BEND SINISTER—An ordinary resembling the bend in form, but extending from the sinister chief to the dexter base. The diminutives of the bend sinister are the *scarpe,* which is half it's width; and the *baton,* half as wide as the scarpe and couped.

IN BEND—When bearings are placed bendwise the term *in bend* is used.

PER BEND—[See *party per bend,* under *Party.*]

Bending—The same as BENDY. *(Chaucer.)*

Bendlet—A diminutive of the bend. Generally it is half the width of the bend; but sometimes it appears much narrower. In ancient heraldry a *bendlet azure* on a a coat was a mark of cadency.

"Bendlets are occasionally enhanced or placed in chief sinister."—*(Glos. of Her.)*

Bendy—An escutcheon having bends which divide it diagonally into four, six or more parts is called *bendy.* The lines are drawn in the same direction described under BEND: when drawn in the contrary direction they are styled *bendy sinister.*

BENDY BARRY—See *Barry Bendy.*

BENDY LOZENGY—Having each lozenge placed in bend.

BENDY PILEY—Divided into an equal number of pieces by piles placed bendwise across the escutcheon.

Beque—(Bee'-kay) Beaked. This term is used of a bird having its bill of a color different from that of the body. [See BEAKED.]

BEQUE.

Bevelled—[See BEVILLED.]

Bevilled—(Bev'-illed) When the outward lines of an ordinary turn in a sloping direction.

BEVILLED.

Bevilways—At a bevil. This term is used of charges or anything similar.

Bezant—(Be-zant') A gold roundlet, representing a coin of that name. It is supposed to have been introduced into English heraldry by the Crusaders, who had received the gold coin while in the East.

BEZANTS.

[See also ROUNDEL..]

[For *Cross Bezant*, see under CROSS.]

Bezante—(Be-zan'-tay) Covered or studded with bezants; semé of bezants.

Bicapitated — (By-cap'-i-ta-ted) Having two heads, such as the two-headed eagle on the arms of Russia, as well as on those of Austria.

Bicorporate — (By-cor'-por-ate) Having two bodies: having the hinder parts in duplicate, with one head and one pair of forepaws.

Big—[See BIGG.]

Bigg—Barley. Specifically, the barley common in the north of Scotland, having six rows of seed. Bigland of Bigland bore "Azure, two ears of bigg or." (Also written big.)

Billhead—The head of a bill. Generally borne on a charge. (The bill was a war instrument—a species of halberd.)

Billet—(Bill'-et) (1) An oblong square, supposed to represent a sheet of paper folded in the form of a letter. Its proportion is two squares.

BILLET.

(2) A staff as a billet, raguled and tricked, meaning a ragged staff in pale. (*Gloss. of Her.*)

Billetty—(Bill'-et-ty) Semé of billets.

BILLETTY COUNTER-BILLETTY — Barry and paly, the divisions of the former being as wide again as those of the latter.

Bird—Birds figure to a large extent in heraldry, and represent the contemplative as well as active life. Among those used with the greatest frequency are the following:

Eagle,	Sheldrake,
Falcon,	Raven,
Swan,	Rook,
Peacock,	Owl,
Pelican,	Cock,
Ostrich,	Popinjay,
Stork,	Cough,
Heron,	Shoveller,
Cormorant,	Swallow.

Among the terms applied to birds are Membered, Armed, Closed, Disclosed, Rising and Volant.

BIRD AND BANTLING — A Lancashire term, applied to the well-known crest of the Stanleys of an eagle preying on a child.

Bird-bolt—A short arrow with a broad, flat end.

BIRD-BOLT.

Bitted—Said of a horse when borne with a bit of a different tincture from the animal itself, when it is said to be *bitted of* that color. This term is also used to describe a horse's head with bit and rein; as, "Three horses' heads couped, bitted and reined or."

Black—This color in heraldry is known as SABLE.

Blackamoor—A negro. Channing of Foxcote bore: "Argent, three blackamoors' heads couped sable, capped or, fretty gules."

Bladed—(Bla'ded) A term used when the stalk of any grain is of a color different from the ear.

Blanch—White. [ARGENT.]
"Nor who, in field or foray slack,
Saw the blanche lion e'er fall black?"
—*Scott: Lay of the Last Minstrel*

Blasted—When a tree is leafless it is said to be *blasted*.

Blaze—To emblazon; to blazon. (Contracted from blazon.)

Blazing star—A comet.

Blazon—(Bla'-zon) To describe a coat of arms; to give an accurate description.
"Proceed unto the beasts that are given in arms, and teach me what I ought to observe in their blazon."—*Peacham*.
"The coat of arms of which I am not herald enough to blazon into English."—*Addison*.
¶ The word blazon comes from the German word *blasen*, to blow as with a horn,

because in the age of heraldry the style and arms of each knight were so proclaimed on public occasions.

Blazoned—That which is blazoned; a blazoned coat of arms.
"Now largesse, largesse, Lord Marmion,
Knight of the crest of gold!
A blazoned shield, in battle won."
—*Scott: Marmion.*

Blazoner—One who blazons coats of arms.

Blazonry—The art of blazoning; to describe a coat of arms in the technical language of heraldry. The rules of blazon are remarkable for their precision, simplicity, brevity and completeness. The proper order of describing arms is: First, give the field, its color (or arrangement of colors, if more than one), and the character of partition lines when parted; second, the charges, and first those of most importance, their name, number and position (when an animal, its attitude); third, marks of difference, cadency, baronet's badge, etc.

Blazure—[From BLAZON.]
"The blazure of his armes was gules."
Berners: Froissart, chap. 281.

Blemish—[See BLEMISHED.]

Blemished—(Blem'-ished) Having an abatement or rebatement. (Used of a sword with its point broken.)

Blighted—The same as BLASTED.

Block Brush—A bunch of the plant Butcher's Broom *(Ruscus aculeatus)*. It is borne by the butchers' company of London.

Blood Color—Sanguine. (Not to be confused with BLOODY.)

Bloody—Gules.

Bloody Hand—A hand tinctured gules. The device of Ulster, hence borne by baronets.

Blue—This color in heraldry is known as AZURE.

Blue Mantle—One of the pursuivants in the College of Arms.

Boar—The boar is one of the ancient charges of heraldry. With the exception of the lion, it is the only beast borne in the roll of Henry III.

Boltant—(Bolt'-ant) Bolting; springing forward. (Used of a hare or rabbit.)

Bolting—[See BOLTANT.]

Bomb-shell—A fire-ball; a projectile of oval shape.

Bonnet—The velvet cap within a coronet.

Border—[See BORDURE.]

Bordure—(Bor'-dure) The border of an escutcheon, occupying one-fifth of the shield. It is sometimes the mark of a younger branch of a family; and, again, when charged, may refer to maternal descent, especially in ancient heraldry. When used in an impaled coat the bordure is not continued around the inner side.

BORDURE.

"In blazoning arms the bordure is placed over all ordinaries except the chief, the quarter and the canton. It has no diminutives, but may at times be surmounted by another of half its width. When a bordure is bezanté, billetté or has similar markings, the number of bezants or billets, unless otherwise mentioned, is always eight."—(Gloss. of Her.)

BORDER COMPONY—This should be composed of 16 pieces. It implies augmentation, or, in more recent times, illegitimacy.

Bote-roll—The same as CRAMPIT.

Bottoned—(Bot'-toned) Having bottonies, buttons, round buds or knots. They are generally displayed in threes. The term is essentially the same as treffled (trefoiled).

Bottony—(Bot'-ton-y) A bud-like projection, of which three are generally together.

CROSS BOTTONY—A cross of which each limb terminates in three bud-like prominences, presenting a slight resemblance to the trefoil.

CROSS BOTTONY.

Bouget—(Bou'-jet) A bucket for carrying water. It is an early charge, and is identified with the names of Ros and Rose. [See WATER BUDGET.]

Bourdonnee—(boor'-don-nay') With the extremity shaped like the handle of a pilgrim's staff; as, a cross bourdonnée. This was the original cross on the arms of Jerusalem, now blazoned "A cross potent."

Bow—The bow occurs in heraldry occasionally, though not as frequently as might have been expected, considering it was once an essential weapon of war.

Boxon—The same as BIRD-BOLT.

Braced—Interlaced. (Also written brased.)

BRACED.

Bracelet—The same as BARRULET.

Braxed—Braced; interlaced. [INTERFRETTED.]

Bretage—(Bret'-ig) Having embattlements on each side.

Brick—Somewhat resembling a billet, but showing its thickness in perspective.

BRICKS.

Broad Arrow—The head represents a pheon, except the engrailing, or jagging, on the inner edge is wanting.

Brock—[See BADGER.]

Broom Plant—The badge of the Plantagenets.

Budget—[See WATER BUDGET.]

Buffaloe—A name applied by some of the earlier writers to the common bull.

Buffler—A wild bull.

Bullet—(Bul'-let) A name sometimes given to the ogress or pellet.

Bute—One of the pursuivants of the Lord Lyon's Court, Scotland.

C.

Cabled—The same as CABLEE.

CROSS CABLEE.

"Cabled is applied to a cross formed of the two ends of a ship's cable; sometimes also to a cross covered over with rounds of rope; more properly called a cross corded."—*Rees: Cyclopedia.*

Cablee—A cross composed of two cable ends.

Caboched—See [CABOSHED.]

Caboshed—(ka-bosht') The head of a beast borne full-faced, and without any neck showing.

"Caboched, caboshed or cabossed * * * is where the head of a beast is cut off behind the ears by a section parallel to the face; or by a perpendicular section, in contradistinction to couped, which is done by a horizontal line; besides that, it is farther from the ears than cabossing. The head, in this case, is placed full-faced, or affrontée, so that no part of the neck can be visible. This bearing is by some called trunked."—*Reese: Cyclopedia.*

Cabossed—[See CABOSHED.]

Cadence—(Ca'-dence) The different steps in the descent of a family.

Cadency—(Ca'-den-cy) As the original object of armorial bearings was to distinguish one iron-encased warrior from

MARKS OF CADENCY.

another, it was also necessary to provide distinctive bearings for different members of a family all entitled to bear the paternal arms. This gave rise to the use of *Marks of Cadency*, or differences (called by the French *brisure*.) They are as follows:

1—Lable,	6—Fleur-de-lis,
2—Crescent,	7—Rose,
3—Mullet,	8—Cross Moline,
4—Martlet,	9—Octofoil.
5—Annulet,	

The eldest son (during the lifetime of his father) bears a lable of three points; the second son, a crescent; the third, a mullet; the fourth, a martlet; the fifth, an annulet; the sixth, a fleur-de-lis; the seventh, a rose; the eighth, a cross moline; the ninth, an octofoil. A younger son of a younger son places a mark upon a mark. Thus the ninth son of a ninth son would place an octofoil upon an octofoil.

Cadet—A younger brother; a junior branch of a family.

Calf—The Calf appears in heraldry occasionally. Le Vele of Tortworth bore "Argent, on a bend sable three calves or," and Calverley, "Argent, on a fesse gules three calves or."

Calthrop—(Cal'-throp) An implement of war, four-spiked, and when thrown on the ground one point always stood upright. Also known as caltrop and chevaltrap.

CALTHROP.

Caltrap—[See CALTHROP.]

Calvary Cross—A cross mounted on three steps. The steps allude to the three Christian graces—Faith, Hope and Charity.

Camelopardel — (Cam-el-o-par'-del) An imaginary beast, with neck and head like a camel, spotted like a pard, with two straight horns similar to those of a giraffe.

Campane—(Cam-pa'ne) A bell; a bell-shaped object.

Campaned—(Cam-pa'ned) Bearing bells, or furnished with bells. (Campane and Campaned are terms that are little used.)

Cannet—(Can'-net) A charge of ducks represented without beaks or feet.

Canting Arms—The same as *Allusive Arms*, which see, under ARMS.

Canton—(Can'-ton) A division of the field placed in the upper dexter corner. It is classed by some heraldic writers as one of the honorable ordinaries; but, strictly speaking, it is a diminutive of the Quarter, being two-thirds the area of that ordinary. However, in the roll of Henry III the quarter appears in several coats which in later rolls are blazoned as cantons. The canton, like the quarter, is an early bearing, and is always shown with straight lines.

CANTON.

CANTON SINISTER—A canton placed on the sinister side of the shield.

Cantoned — (Can'-toned) Applied to a shield in which the four spaces around a cross or saltier are filled with any pieces.

Cap of Maintenance—The cap of state carried before a sovereign at his coronation. Occasionally used as a bearing on a shield.

Cat—The Cat figures in heraldry as the Musion, the Catamount, Cat-a-mountain, Wildcat and just plain cat.

The Keate family bore "Argent, three mountain cats passant in pale sable."

The musion was the emblem of Burgundy, and, according to a fable of the day, the arms of an imprisoned cat were granted to the knight who took prisoner Gundemar of Burgundy.

Catamount—[See CAT.]

Cat-a-mountain—[See CAT.]

Chabot—[See CHALBOT.]

Chafant—(Chaf'-ant) Applied to a boar when depicted as enraged.

Chain—The chain was borne by the kings of Navarre, the arms being blazoned: "Gules, a trellis of chains or, in cross saltire."

Chalbot—(shal'-bot) The heraldic name of the fish commonly known as Bullhead or Miller's Thumb.

Chamber—The cylindrical part of ordnance is blazoned as Chamber. Example: "Three chambers sable, fired proper."

Champ—The field or ground of a field. "The champe of his field was gules."— *Lydgate.*

Champain—(Cham'-pain) A mark of dishonor in the coat of arms of one who has killed an opponent after he has asked for quarter.

Chancellor—A functionary in an order of knighthood. For example, the Chancellor of the Order of the Garter, who acts in the capacity of secretary of that order.

Chapeau—(shap'-o) A cap of state borne by a duke.

Chaperon—(shap'-er-on) An ornamental hood worn by the Knights of the Garter when in full dress.

Chaperonnet—(shap-er-on'-net) A small hood.

Chapournet—(shap-our'-net) A chaperonnet borne in arms dividing the chief by a bow-shaped line.

CHAPOURNET.

Chaplet—A garland or wreath; a head band of leaves borne in coats of arms in token of great military prowess. The chaplet made its first appearance in the roll of Edward II.

Charge—To place upon an escutcheon.

Charge—Anything occupying the field in an escutcheon. There are two kinds of charges—proper and common.

PROPER CHARGES—So called because they peculiarly belong to the art of heraldry. [See *ordinary.*]

COMMON CHARGES—Those charges which have been imported into heraldry from all quarters, representing an array of objects, natural and artificial, from reptiles and insects to the human being and celestial figures.

"The charge is that which is borne upon the color, except it be a coat divided only by partition."—*Peacham.*

Charged—A charge placed upon the field.

Chausse—(sho'-say) This term denotes a section in base formed by a line from the extremity of the base ascending to the side of the escutcheon, joining it at about the fesse point.

Checky—(check'-y) A field divided into small squares, of different tinctures, resembling a chess-board. Usually made up of seven squares in the top line, and in depth according to the length of the shield.

CHECKY.

Checquy—[See CHECKY.]

Chess-rook—A bearing which resembles

the rook, or castle, in chess.

CHESS-ROOK.

Chester—One of the heralds of the College of Arms.

Cheval Trap—[See CALTHROP.]

Chevalier—(shev'-a-lier)   A horseman armed at all points.

Cheveron—[See CHEVRON.]

Chevron—(shev'-ron) One of the honorable ordinaries. It is rafter-shaped, and its breadth is one-fifth of the field. Its diminutives are the *Chevronel*, which is one-fifth of its breadth ; and the *Couple-close*, one-quarter. When repeated up to three they may be chevrons or chevronels; exceeding three, the bearing is chevronny, unless the number is specified.

CHEVRON.

CHEVRON COUPED—Applied to a chevron which does not reach the sides of an escutcheon.

CHEVRON IN CHIEF—One which rises to the top of the shield.

Chevronel—(shev'-ron-el) A diminutive of the chevron, being half its breadth.

Chevronne—[See CHEVRONNY.]

Chevronny—(shev'-ron-ny) A shield laid out in partitions chevronwise.

Chief—The head or upper part of the shield, containing a third of the field, and is divided off by one line, either straight or crenellé (indented). When one chief is borne upon another it is called surmounting.

CHIEF.

IN CHIEF—Anything borne in the chief.

ON CHIEF—When the chief is charged with anything.

Chief Point—The uppermost part of the shield, and can be either *dexter, middle* or *sinister*.

Chimæra—(ki-me'-ra) A modification of some existing animal, such as the winged lion of St. Mark, the dragon, etc.

Chough—(shuff) [See AYLET.]

Cinquefoil — (sink'-foil) A five-pointed leaf ; usually borne without a stem.

Clarenceux—(Clar'-en-saw) The title of the second King-of-Arms. He ranks next to Garter.

Clarion—(klar'-i-un) An instrument somewhat resembling a trumpet. The clarion borne by Granville, however, resembles the pan-pipe.

Cleche—(clay'-shay) A cross charged with another of the same design, but having the same color as the field, leaving only a narrow border of the first cross visible. (Can be used of other bearings.) [Compare with VOIDED.]

CROSS CLECHE.

Clouee—(klu'ay) [French.] Said of the fretty when nailed at the joints.

Close—The wings of a bird close to the body.

Closed—Applied to a bird borne with wings folded close to the body.

Closet—A diminutive of the bar, being one-quarter the breadth of that bearing.

Closeted—Inclosed within closets; supplied with closets.

Coambulant—Walking together.

Coat—*Coat of Arms, Coat-Armor, Cote-Armure*, etc.—Originally armorial bearings were embroidered on the surcoat of the wearer. The term is now used for the escutcheon, or shield, when arms are displayed. [For further information on coats of arms see ARMS.]

Cock—This fowl is generally borne as a crest, but occasionally appears on the shield. When the beak, comb, wattles and spur are given, he is said to be beaked, wattled (or jewlapped) and armed.

Cockatrice—A fabulous animal supposed to have been produced from a cock's egg hatched by a serpent. [See BASILISK.]

Co-erectant—(co-erect'-ant) Applying to things set up side by side.

Cœur—The heart of the shield. The same as the center or fesse point.

Cognizance—[See BADGE.]

Collar—An ornament for the neck worn by a knight or other member as a badge of that order.

Collared—The same as GORGED.

College of Arms—(Or *Heralds' College*) is located on Queen Victoria street, E. C., London, a royal corporation founded by King Richard III. It consists at present of the Earl Marshal, his secretary, a Registrar, three Kings at Arms—Garter, Clarenceux and Norry—and the following Heralds: Chester, Lancashire, York, Somerset, Richmond and Windsor. There are also four Pursuivants—Rouge Croix, Bluemantle, Rouge Dragon and Portcullis—besides various other officers. This institution determines all questions relating to arms and grants of armorial bearings. The office of Earl Marshal is now hereditary, being held by the Dukes of Norfolk. The corresponding college for Scotland is know as Lyon Court, and that of Ireland Office of Arms.

Color—For the colors of heraldry see TINCTURE.

Combatant—(com'-bat-ant) A term applied to beasts borne face to face, as in the attitude of fighting.
  (Also written *Combattant.*)

COMBATANT.

Community—*Arms of Community*. [See under ARMS.

Companion—A term applied to a certain grade of members in some of the knightly orders, as, a Companion of the Bath.

Companionship—The rank of a knight companion of certain orders.

Compartment—The partitions and quarterings of the escutcheon according to the coat in it.

Compone—[See COMPONY.]

Componed—[See COMPONY.]

Compony—(com-po'ny) A border, bend, etc., composed of a row of squares consisting of colors and metals. (Sometimes written *componé.*)

COMPONY.

COMPONY COUNTER-COMPONY—The same as above, but arranged in two rows.

Composed—*Arms Composed* are the addition by a gentleman to his own armorial bearings of a portion of those borne by his wife. The practice is now obsolete, the device of marshalling the arms of one's wife with his own having rendered its continuance unnecessary. *(Gloss. of Her.)*

Concaved—When ordinaries, etc., are bowed in the form of an arch they are sometimes referred to as *concaved.*

Concession—*Arms of Concession.* [See under ARMS.]

Confronte—(kon'-frun'-tay') Face to face; two animals facing each other.

CONFRONTE.

Conger—(kon'-ger) An eel. Specifically, the large sea eel found on the coast of Britain.

Contourne—(kon'-toor'-nay') [French.] Turned in a direction not the usual one. Applied to a lion or other animal statant, passant, courant, etc., with its face to the sinister side of the escutcheon. (Some writers use the word "counter" in this sense.)

Contre—(con'-tre) [French] Used, in composition, to describe several bearings when they cut the shield in a contrary and opposite manner. Example: *Contre-chevron,* alluding to two chevrons opposite to each other—where color opposes metal and metal opposes color.

Contey—(co'-ney) This is the heraldic rabbit. (Also written cony, coni, conni and conig.)

Corbeau—The same as CORBIE.

Corbie—(kor'-by) A raven; a crow. (Also written CORBY.)

Corby—The same as CORBIE.

Cordal—(cord'-al) A string of the robe of state, composed of silk and gold threads, twisted like a cord, and having a tassel at the end.

Corded—Bound or wound round with cords.

Cordon—(cor'-don) A ribbon worn across the breast by knights of some orders.

Cork—One of the heralds of the Office of Arms, Ireland.

Corned—When the horns of a beast, such as the bull, are of a different tincture from that of the body he is then said to be *corned of* that tincture. [See ARMED 3.]

Cornished—(corn'-ished) Adorned with a cornish or molding.

Coronet—An inferior sort of crown worn by nobles. The Prince of Wales' coronet consists of a circle of gold, jeweled, edged above with four crosses patée and as many fleur-de-lis, and closed with four bars and an orb and cross. A duke's coronet is bordered with eight strawberry leaves; that of a marquis with four, alternating with four pearls; that of an earl has eight strawberry leaves alternating with eight pearls; the viscount uses pearls only, but of an indefinite number, while the baron is restricted to four pearls only.

¶ The bishops of England have no coronet, but ensign their arms with a mitre.

Cost—One of the subordinaries, being a diminutive of the bend. When borne in pairs it is called Cottise.

Cotise—[See COTTISE.]

Cotised—[See COTTISED.]

Cottise—(cot'-tise) The same as COST.

Cottised—(cot'-tised) A term applied to ordinaries when borne between two cottises.

Couchant—(couch'-ant) Applied to an animal lying down, with head raised.

COUCHANT.

¶ This term differs from *dormant* in that in the latter sense the beast is represented sleeping.

Couche—(coo-shey') [French.] Said of anything lying sideways, as a *chevron couché*=a chevron placed sideways.

Counter—In an opposite direction; contrary to the usual position. Sometimes used to denote an animal facing the sinister side of the shield. [In this sense see *Contourné*.]

COUNTER-ATTIRED—Applied to the double horns of animals when borne two one way and two another—in opposite directions.

COUNTER-CHEVRONNE — Chevronny divided palewise. (Said of the field.) The equivalent of chevronné, of chevronny.

COUNTER-COMPONY—A border, bend, etc., which is composed of two rows of checkers of alternate tinctures.

COUNTER-COUCHANT—Animals borne couchant, their heads being in opposite directions.

COUNTER-COURANT—Said of two animals borne courant, and with their heads in opposite directions.

COUNTER-EMBATTLED—Applied to an ordinary embattled on both sides.

COUNTER-ERMINE—The contrary of ermine, being a black field with white spots. [See *Ermines.*]

COUNTER-FLEURY—A term used to show that the flowers adorning an ordinary stand opposite to each other.

COUNTER-PASSANT—Applied to two animals borne passant going in contrary ways.

COUNTER-POTENCE — Said of potences when placed opposite each other.

COUNTER-QUARTERED—When each quarter of an escutcheon is again quartered.

COUNTER-SALIENT—Applied to two animals borne salient in opposite directions.

COUNTER-TRIPPANT—Animals trippant in opposite directions.

COUNTER-TRIPPING—The same as *Counter-trippant.*

COUNTER-VAIR—A variety of vair, in which the cups or bells are arranged base to base and point to point.

COUNTER-VAIRY—The same *Counter-vair.*

Counterchanged—A term which denotes that the field is of two tinctures, metal and color; that part of the charge which lies in the metal being of color, and that part which lies in the color being metal.

Counterpaled—A term used of an escutcheon which is divided into an equal number of pieces palewise by a line fessewise, the tinctures above and below the fesse line being counterchanged.

Counterpointe—(-point-é) Made use of to describe two chevrons which meet with their points in the center of the shield, counter to each other. (The French use *contrepointé.)*

COUNTERPOINTE.

Couped—(koop'd) Said of an animal having the head or any limb cut clean off from the body.

¶ A head couped is a head having the appearance of being cut off with a sharp knife.

COUPED.

Couple-close—One of the diminutives of the chevron, being one-quarter the breadth of that ordinary. It is borne in pairs, inclosing the chevron. (Sometimes written couple-closs.)

Couple-closed—Inclosed by the couple-close; as, "A chevron couple-closed."

Coward—Said of beasts represented with the tail between the legs.

Crampit—The cramp-iron of a scabbard.

Cramponee—(cramp-on'-ay) A cross having at each end a cramp or crampoon.

CRAMPONEE.

Crenellated—(cre'-nel-la-ted) An ordinary indented as with crenelles.

Crescent—A bearing resembling the half moon with the points turned up. When used as a mark of cadency it denotes the second son.

CRESCENT.

¶ When the points of the crescent face dexter it is *increscent;* toward sinister, *decrescent.*

Crest—Originally the crest was the orna-

CREST.

ment of the helmet, or headpiece, and also afforded protection against a blow. In the early roles it was scarcely noticed, but in later armorial grants it came into general use. Crests, like arms, were sometimes allusive. Thus, Grey of Wilton used a gray, or badger, and Lord Wells a bucket and chain. In the early days of the crest it was confined to persons of rank, but in latter times it has been included in every grant of arms.

¶ A coronet or helmet below the crest is not a mark of rank.

Crined—Used to describe an animal having its hair of a different tincture.

Croisant—(crois'-ant) A cross the ends of which terminate in crescents.

Cross—One of the earliest and noblest of the honorable ordinaries. When borne plain it is blazoned simply as a cross. There are, however, more than a hundred varieties, some of the better known being the following:

Anchored,	Fitchee,
Avellane,	Flory,
Bezant,	Formee,
Bottony,	Moline,
Cablee,	Patee,
Calvary,	Potent,
Chain,	Recercelee,
Cleche,	Voided.
Crosslet,	

Cross Anchored—A cross in which the limbs terminate in anchors.

CROSS ANCHORED.

Cross Avellane—Ending in filbert husks.

Cross Bezant—A cross composed of bezants joined together.

Cross Bottany—With the limbs terminating in budlike prominences.

CROSS BOTTONY.

Cross Cablee—A cross made up of two cables.

CROSS CABLEE.

Cross Corded—A cross bound or wound round with cords. (This term is sometimes applied, though erroneously, to the Cablée.)

Cross Cleche—A cross charged with another cross, of the same color of the field, so large that only a narrow border of the first cross remains visible.

Cross Crosslet—A cross having the three upper ends terminating in three little crosses. It is usualy borne in num-

CROSS CROSSLET.

bers, but this is not always the case.

CROSS FITCHEE—Sharpened at the lower part; pointed like a dagger. The arms of the See of Canterbury represent four crosses patée fitchée.

CROSS FITCHEE.

CROSS FLEURY—Adorned at the ends with flowers, generally the fleur-de-lis.

CROSS FOURCHEE—Having the ends forked as branches, with the ends terminating abruptly, as if cut off.

CROSS FOURCHEE.

CROSS FORMEE—Resembling the cross patée, but differing in that its extremities reach the edge of the field.

CROSS MOLINE—So called because its shape resembles a millrind (the iron clamp of the upper millstone). It is borne both inverted and rebated, and sometimes saltirewise or in saltire. When used as a mark of cadency it represents the eighth son.

CROSS OF CALVARY (or *Cross of the Crucifixion*)—Represented mounted on three steps.

CROSS OF ST. GEORGE—A plain red cross on a white field. It would be blazoned "Argent, a cross gules."

CROSS PATEE — The emblem of the Knights of St. John, and is known as the Croix de Malthe. It spreads out at the ends.

CROSS PATONCE—This has expanded ends like the cross patée, but each terminates in three points.

CROSS POMMEE—With the ends terminating in single balls.

CROSS POMMEE.

CROSS POTENT—One which has its ends T-shaped, or resembling a crutch. (Also written potence.)

CROSS RAGULY—A notched or jagged cross.

CROSS RAGULY.

CROSS RECERCELEE — A cross whose ends are split and curled outward. It is usually voided.

CROSS URDEE—Differs from an ordinary cross only in that the extremities are drawn to a sharp point instead of being cut straight.

CROSS VOIDED—A cross in outline only.

Cross-bar—Sometimes used to designate the bar sinister; a mark of illegitimacy.

Crossbow—[See ARBLAST.]

Crossed—Borne crosswise.

Crosswise—In the figure of a cross. (Essentially the same as CROSSED.)

Crown—The crown of a sovereign prince is usually closed at the top by four arched bars, called diadems, and surmounted by a globe and cross.

¶ A crown placed below the crest does not denote the rank of the bearer.

IRON CROWN—A crown which, besides its gold and jewels, contains a thin circle of iron, said to have been made from a nail of Christ's cross. It was first used at the coronation of the Lombard kings in A. D. 591. Napoleon I was crowned with it at Milan in 1805.

Crowned—Surmounted by a crown. Sometimes a beast, generally the lion, is crowned royally or ducally.

Crucilly—(cru'sil-ly) Said of a charge or field strewn with crosses.

Crusade—One of several expeditions of Christian knights against the Mohammedans in the Holy Land. There were seven distinct crusades.

Crusader—One who took part in the crusades.

Cubit arm—An arm cut off at the elbow.

Cuppa—(kup'-pa) A fur composed of any metal and color. Also called *Potent-counter-potent.*

Currant—The same as courant. *(Universal Dict.)*

Curvant—(kurv'-ant) Curved; bowed.

Cygnet royal—(sig'-net) A swan gorged

CYGNET ROYAL.

with a ducal coronet, and a chain attached thereto, being reflexed over the back.

D.

Damasked—(dam'-askd) A field or charge covered with small squares. [See DIAPER.]

Dancette—(daṇ'-sa'-tay') Divided into large zigzags; resembling the zigzag molding peculiar to Norman architecture.

¶ Dancetté differs from *indented in* that the former has deeper and wider notches.

Dancy—(dan'sy) The same as DANCETTE.

Dauphin—(dau'-fin) [French.] The title of the eldest son of the king of France or the heir apparent to the throne under the old monarchy. [DOLPHIN.]

¶ The title is said to have come from the following circumstance: Humbert II Lord of Vinne, who bore for a crest a dolphin (O. Fr. *daulphin*), in the ninth century, bequeathed his lordship as an appanage to the French throne on condition that the eldest son always bore the title of Dauphin of Viennois.

Debased—Turned over; inverted.

DEBASED HERALDRY—Unheraldic. There are a number of examples that could be placed under this head. For instance, one grant of arms shows negroes working on a plantation; another has Chinamen carrying cinnamon; a Bishop of Ely bore, among other things, three kings, on bezants, crowned, robed sable, doubled ermine, a covered cup in the right hand and a sword in the left, both or; the grant to Lord Nelson, as well as some of his officers, were altogether unheraldic.

Debruised—(de-bruzd') Applied to a bend when placed over an animal in such a manner as to seem to restrain its freedom.

DEBRUISED.

Dechausse—(day-sho'-say) [French.] The same as DISMEMBERED.

Decked—Said of a bird when its feathers are trimmed or edged with a small line of another color.

Declinant—(dek'-lin-ant) Used in describing a serpent whose tail is represented straight downward. (Also called Declivant.)

Declivant—(dek'-liv-ant) The same as DECLINANT.

Decouple—(de-koup'-lay) [French.] Parted; severed. (The same as UNCOUPLED.)

Decrement—(dec're-ment) The wane of the moon from full to last quarter. [See DECRESCENT.]

Decrescent—(de-kres'-sent) Said of the moon when in her decrement. When the crescent is borne with its points toward the sinister side of the shield it is termed *decrescent*.

Defamed—An epithet applied to an animal which has lost its tail.

Degraded—This word describes a cross

CROSS DEGRADED AND CONJOINED.

that has steps at each end, diminishing as they ascend toward the center.

CROSS DEGRADED AND CONJOINED—A plain cross having degraded steps joined to the sides of the shield.

Delf—One of the abatements; a mark of disgrace, indicating that a challenge has been revoked or one's word broken. The delf is represented by a square-cut sod of earth, turf, etc. [See also ABATEMENT.]

Delve—(delv) The same as BILLET.

Demembre—(da-mem'-bray) [French.] The same as DISMEMBERED.

Demi—Said of any charge borne half, as a demi-lion. (Also written demy.)

Demi-garter—[See PERCLOSE.]

Dent—Indented. *(Universal Dict.)*

Dentelle—(den-tel') [French.] The same as INDENTED.

Depressed—The same as DEBRUISED.

Descending—Said of an animal or bird the head of which is represented turned toward the base of the shield.

Descent—Coming down from above. Example: A lion *in descent*=with his head toward the base point and his heels toward one of the corners of the chief, as if in the act of leaping down from some high place.

Detriment—(det'-ri-ment) Used sometimes to describe the moon on the wane or in eclipse.

Developed—Unfurled, as colors flying.

Device—An emblem, intended to represent a family, person, action or quality, with a suitable motto. It generally consists in a metaphorical similitude between the thing representing and the person or thing represented.

Devouring—The same as VORANT.

Dexter—The right; situated on the right. The dexter side of the shield is that opposite the left hand of the spectator.

DEXTER CHIEF POINT—A point in the upper right-hand corner of the shield.

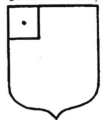

DEXTER CHIEF POINT.

Diaper—(di'-a-per) A ground pattern, usually in squares or lozenges.

Diapered—(di'-a-perd) A shield diapered is one covered with a ground pattern, generally of squares or lozenges, with a flower scroll work or other ornament in each compartment. The idea is supposed to have been copied from the linen cloths of Ypress.

DIAPERED.

¶ While there are a number of early examples of diapered shields, it cannot be called strictly heraldic.

Diadem—An arch rising from the rim of a crown and uniting with other arches to form a center, which serves to support the globe and cross or fleur-de-lis as a crest.

Difference—Some figure of mark added

MARKS OF DIFFERENCE.

to a coat of arms to distinguish one family from another. Modern marks of difference, or *Marks of Cadence*, are:

1—Lable,	6—Fleur-de-lis,
2—Crescent,	7—Rose,
3—Mullet,	8—Cross Moline,
4—Martlet,	9—Octofoil.
5—Annulet,	

Differenced—Marked or distinguished by a difference.

Dimidiate—(di-mid'-i-ate) To represent the half of any charge.

Dimidiation—[See DIMIDIATE.]

Diminution—(di-mi-nu'-shon) The defacing of some particular point in an escutcheon.

Diminutive — (di-min'-u-tive) Something smaller than the regular size; on a smaller scale. For instance, the diminutive of the *Bend* is the *Bendlet*, being half its width.

Dingwall—One of the pursuivants of the Lord Lyon's Court, Scotland.

Disarmed—Applied to a bird or beast deprived of claws, teeth or beak.

Disclosed—A term used to describe a bird when its wings are spread open on each side, but the points downward.

DISCLOSED.

DISCLOSED ELEVATED—The same as disclosed, except that the points are elevated.

Dismembered—Applied to birds having neither feet nor legs; also, to animals whose members are separated.

Displayed—Said of any bird of prey borne

erect, with the wings expanded. Applied especially to the eagle.

DISPLAYED.

¶ This term is not to be confused with DISCLOSED.

Distillatory—(dis-til'-la-tory) A charge borne by the Distillers' Company, and usually blazoned : "A distillatory double armed, on a fire, with two worms and bolt receivers." *(Ogilvie.)*

¶The distillatory is an apparatus used for distillation.

Disveloped—(dis-vel'-opd) Displayed, as a standard or colors when open and flying. *(Universal Dict.)*

Dog—The dog figures in heraldry in various forms and under different names. The alaund, or hunting dog, seems to have been the most popular. Lord Dacre used it as a supporter. Henry VIII had his arms and badge placed on the collars of his hunting dogs. In the brass of Sir Brian Stapleton at Ingham the knight rests his foot on a dog. The earls of Shrewsbury use the talbot, or mastiff, to support their shield. Burton of Falde bore three talbots' heads erased or, while Mauleverer of Allerton Mauleverer had three greyhounds on his shield.

¶ The dog is generally blazoned as a *talbot.*

Dolphin—(dol'-fin) The dolphin is heraldically a fish, irregardless of what it may be zoologically or astronomically. When used as a charge it may be extended and natant or haurlant, etc. Fishacre of Fishacre bore "Gules, a dolphin natant argent." The dolphin was the emblem of the Dauphins of France. [See also DAUPHIN.]

Dominion—[See *Arms of Dominion,* under ARMS.]

Dormant—In a sleeping posture.

DORMANT.

Dorsed—The same as AVERSANT.

Doubling—The lining of robes of state ; also the mantlings borne around the achievement of arms.

Dragon—The dragon is of ancient date and played a prominent part in early romance, though little used in English heraldry. He is usually depicted with four legs and wings, a long barbed tail, usually knotted, and a body protected by scales. When the dragon is drawn without wings he is called a lindworm ; without feet, a serpent ; when he hangs by the head, it represents a conquered dragon.

Dragonnee—(dra-gon'-nay) A fabulous beast, the upper part resembling a lion, and the lower part the wings and tail of a dragon.

Drops—The same as GUTTES.

Dublin—One of the heralds of the Office of Arms, Ireland.

Ducal coronet—The head attire of a duke, consisting of a circle of chased gold, with eight strawberry leaves on its upper edge, a cap of crimson velvet, terminating at the top with a gold tassel. When a coronet is used in a crest it is generally the ducal.

Duke—The highest rank in the peerage of Great Britain.

Dwale—(dwal)—The tincture sable, or black, when blazoned according to the fantastic system in which plants are substituted for the tinctures. *(Webster.)*

E.

Eagle—The Eagle plays an important part in heraldry in almost every part of the globe. Its earliest rise to popularity, however, was in Germany, where, after it became the emblem of the empire, it was adopted by some the princes and many of the nobles. A double-headed eagle is also the emblem of Russia and Austria. On the role of Henry III the eagle appears but twice, but in the roll of Edward II there are forty-three example of it. Nobles of the Holy Roman Empire place their shields on the breast of an eagle, examples of which may be seen in the arms of the Duke of Marlborough, the Earl of Denbigh and Lord Arundel of Wardour.

The imperial eagle is invariably represented as two-headed, the origin of which is obscure. Charlemagne is said to have used it to signify that in his hands was the government of both the Roman and German empires.

BICAPITATED.
(Two-headed Eagle.)

The eagle is generally borne displayed; that is, upright, breast to the front, and legs, tail and wings expanded (commonly called a "spread eagle").

¶ The Bald Eagle, adopted as the national emblem of the United States, is a large and powerful bird, with a far greater spread of wing than the European white-tailed species.

Eared—Applied to animals borne with the ears of a different color from that of the body. In such a case the animal is said to be "eared of" such a color or metal.

Earl—The title of an English noble, the third in rank, coming next below a marquis.

EARL'S CORONET—The head attire of an earl, sometimes used in blazonry. The crest of Davidson in Carlisle Cathedral shows a bird rising out of an earl's coronet. This in unusual, however. Generally a ducal coronet is used.

EARL MARSHAL—An English office of great antiquity, and is now hereditary with the Dukes of Norfolk. The Earl Marshal is the head of the College of Arms, which institution determines all questions relating to arms and grants of armorial bearings.

EARL MARSHAL'S COURT—An institution formerly existing in England, presided over by the Earl Marshal, in which all questions and disputes concerning coats of arms were settled. It has since been abolished.

Edged—Applied to an ordinary to denote that the edging is placed only between the ordinary and the field, and not where it joins the escutcheon.

Effare—(af-fa'-ray) [French.] Said of an animal when represented as rearing on its hind legs from fright or rage.

Eight-foil—A grass that has eight leaves. [See OCTOFOIL.]

Elevated—Applied to the wings of a bird when upright and expanded.

Embattled—Indented like a battlement.

EMBATTLED.

The notch in a parapet is called an *embrazure*, and the intermediate piece of masonry a *merlon*. When a second and smaller merlon is placed on the first the battlement is said to be *stopped*.

EMBATTLED COUNTER-EMBATTLED—Embattled on both faces of the ordinary.

EMBATTLED GRADY—One embattlement upon another.

Emblazon—To blazon; to place and arrange figures armorial.

Emblazoner—One who blazons.

Emblazonment—The act or art of blazoning; blazonry.

Emblazonry — Heraldic representations or decorations.

Embordered—(-bor'-derd) having a border of the same tincture as the field.

Embordured—(-bor'-durd) The same as EMBORDERED.

Embowed—(-bow'd) Bent or bowed.

Embraced—Braced together ; bound or tied together.

Embrasure—[See EMBATTLED.]

Embroidery—A term applied to a hill or mount with several copings or rises and falls.

Embrued—(-brud') Said of the mouths of beasts when bloody from devouring their prey ; also applied to a weapon represented as covered or sprinkled with blood.

Emerald—Green. [See VERT.]

✦ **Empaled**—(-paled') This is a term used to describe a shield in which coats of arms are placed side by side, each occupying one-half the escutcheon. The shield is divided by a line down the center (per pale). The arms of the husband are placed on the dexter side, and those of the wife on the sinister. [EMPALEMENT.]

Empalement—Two coats of arms placed on a shield palewise.

Enaluron — (en-a-lu'ron) Applied to a bordure charged with eight birds.

Enarched—Arched.

Enarmed—Represented with horns, hoofs, etc., of a different color from that of the body.

Enclave—(in-kla've) [French.] Anything which is represented as let into something else, particularly when the bearing so let in is square.

Endorse—One of the diminutives of the pale, being one-eighth the breadth of that ordinary. The endorse is used only in pairs—one on each side of the pale. This subordinary, like the pallet, was unknown in ancient heraldry.

Endorsed—A pale having an endorse on each side.

Enfiled—Used to describe a sword drawn as transfixing the head of a man or animal, a coronet or other object.

Englante—(an-glan'-tay) [French.] Bearing acorns or something similar.

Englislet—(eng'-lis-let) An escutcheon of pretense.

Engoulee—(an-goo'-lay) An epithet applied to a bend, cross, saltire, etc., when the ends enter the mouths of lions, tigers or other animals.

ENGOULEE.

Engrail—(-grail') To indent in curved lines : to make ragged at the edges : to spot as with hail.

Engrailed—Indented in a series of curves.

ENGRAILED.

This is applied to one of the partition lines, as well as to some bends, etc.

"Polwheel beareth a saultier engrailed."
—*Carew.*

Engrailment—The state of being engrailed or indented in curved lines.

Enhanced—(en-hansd') Applied to an ordinary when removed from its proper position and placed higher up in the field.

Enleve—(an-lev'-é) [French.] Raised or elevated.

Enmanche—(an-man'-shay) [French.] Covered with or resembling a sleeve. Said when the chief has lines drawn from the center of the upper edge to the sides to about half the breadth of the chief. [MAUNCH.]

Enraged—In a leaping posture. It is sometimes used to describe the position of a horse which in the case of other animals would be saliant.

Ensign—To distinguish by a mark or ornament. such as a crown, coronet, mitre, etc. A bishop. for instance, ensigns his arms with a mitre.

Prelates of the Roman Catholic Church ensign their shields with a hat, the tassels of which indicate their rank. A cardinal has four rows of red tassels, an archbishop four rows of green tassels, a bishop has three rows and an abbot two, the latter's hat being black. Prelates and legates place a patriarchal cross in pale behind their shield.

A staff is sometimes said to be ensigned with a flag.

Ensigned—[See ENSIGN.]

Ente—(an-tay') [French.] Applied to an engrafted emblazonment. (Also written *anté.*)

Entoured—(en-toord') Said of a shield decorated with branches.

Entwined—The same as ENVELOPED.

Entwisted—The same as ENVELOPED.

Enurny—(en-ur'-ny) A term used to describe a bordure charged with eight animals of any kind.

¶ When birds are used *enalurion* is the proper term.

Enveloped—Applied to charges around which serpents are entwined. Also used in the case of laurel or other plants.

Environed—(-vi'-rond) Encircled; bound round or about.

Erased—(e-ras'd) A term applied to the head of an animal or other bearing having the appearance of being forcibly torn off, leaving jagged or uneven ends.

ERASED.

¶ Erased is the opposite of *couped*, the latter meaning cut off even, straight.

Eradicated—A tree torn up by its roots.

Ericius—[See HEDGEHOG.]

Ermelin—[See ERMINE.]

Ermine—(er'-min) One of the furs used in blazoning, representing the skin of the little animal of that name. A field of ermine is white with black spots of a particular shape.

ERMINE.

The animal ermine is scarcely known in heraldry, although its fur is widely borne.

Ermines—The reverse of Ermine, being white spots on a black field. (Sometimes described as counter-ermine.)

Erminites—(er-min'-ites) The same as Ermine, but with one red hair on each side of the ermine spots.

Erminois—(er'-min-wa) The same as Ermine, except that the field is gold and the spots black.

Escarbuncle—(es'-kar-bun-k'l) A charge or bearing supposed to represent the precious stone carbuncle, being a cross of eight rays set with knobs and the arms ending in fleur-de-lis. In another representation of this bearing the ends are connected by cross-bars. (Also called Carbuncle.)

Escallop—es-kol'-up) The figure of a scallop shell. This was originally worn to signify that the wearer had made a pilgrimage to the shrine of St. James, Compostella, Spain. Later on it was placed on the shield to show that the bearer or an ancestor had been a Crusader or had made a long pilgrimage.

Escallopee — (es-kol'-lo-pay) [French.] An escutcheon or a bearing which is covered with curved lines resembling scallop shells. These lines should represent the shells as overlapping each other.

ESCALLOPEE.

Escalloped—(es-kol'-oped) The same as ESCALLOPEE.

Escartel—(es-kar'-tel) To cut or notch in a square form or across.

Escartelee—(-kar'-tel-ée) Cut or notched in a square form or across.

Esclatte—(es-klat'-ty) A term applied to anything shivered by a battle axe.

Escrol—(es-krol') The same as SCROLL.

Escutcheon—(es-kuch'-un) The shield, on which all lines are drawn and charges delineated; the background on which coat armor is represented; known in blazon as the field. It originally represented the war shield of a knight, upon which his arms were displayed.

ESCUTCHEON.

Escutcheon of Pretense—A small shield bearing the arms of an heiress placed in the center of her husband's shield, instead of being impaled with his arms.

Escutcheoned—(es-kuch'-und) Having a coat of arms; supplied with an escutcheon; placed in an escutcheon.

Esquire—Formerly an armor-bearer or attendant upon a knight.

Essorant—(es'-so-rant) Said of a bird represented with its wings half open, as if preparing to take flight.

Estoile—(es'-twal) [French.] A star with six wavy points. It is different from a

ESTOILE

mullet, the later having only five points, and these are straight.

Estoilee—(es'-twal-ée) [French.] A star with four long rays in the form of a cross, tapering from the center to the points. (Also called a *Cross Estoilée*.)

Extendant—(ex-tend'-ant) The same as DISPLAYED. (Wings extended.)

Eyed—A term made use of in speaking of the spots in a peacock's tail.

Eyrant—(i'-rant) Applied to eagles or other birds in their nests.

F.

Faillis—(fáil'-lis) [French.] A fracture in an ordinary, as if it were broken or a splinter taken from it.

Falcon—The Falcon makes its appearance frequently in heraldry. When it is borne with jesses (leather thongs about its legs), a hood and bells, it is said to be "jessed, hooded and belled." When represented as feeding, it is "at prey." The falcon is also known as a gerfalcon, peregrine falcon and tiercelet.

The lure was a bunch of feathers by which the bird was taught to return.

False—Said of a charge when the central area is removed.

Family—*Arms of Family*. [See under ARMS.]

Feathered—Applied to an arrow in which the feather is of a different tincture from the shaft.

Fer de cheval—A horseshoe.

Fer de moline—The same as MILLRIND.

Fess—[See FESSE.]

Fesse—(fes) One of the ordinaries. A

FESSE.

strip or band placed horizontally across the shield, occupying one-third of the field. Its diminutives are the bar, the barrulet and the closet.

¶ The term *fessey* is never used.

FESSE LINE—The line constituting the fesse.

FESSE POINT—The exact center of the shield.

Fesseways—The same as FESSEWISE.

Fessewise—In the sape of a fesse; after the manner of a fesse.

Fetterlock—Sometimes borne as a charge.

FETTERLOCK.
"A fetterlock and a shacklebolt azure—
what may that mean?"—*Ivanhoe.*

Feudal—*Feudal Arms*. [See under ARMS.]

Fiched—[See FITCHEE.]

Field—The surface of a shield upon which the charges or bearings are blazoned; or, of each separate coat when the shield is quartered or impaled.

Fillet—(fil'-let) A bearing equaling in breadth one-fourth of the chief. It is a narrow strip laid upon the chief, a little above its lower margin. Guillim mentions the fillet as the diminutive of the chief.

Fimbriated—(fim'-bri-a-ted) Ornamented with a narrow border or hem of another tincture.

Fireball—A charge resembling the ancient war instrument of that name, which was an oval-shaped projectile made of canvas and filled with combustible composition.

Fish—Fishes do not appear frequently in

heraldry, and are rarely seen in the earlier coats. Among those used are:

Barbel,	Luce,
Chalbot,	Roach,
Conger,	Trout,
Dolphin,	Whale.
Herring,	

[The above are all heraldically fish, irregardless of their position in any other science.]

The fish may be borne *natant*, horizontal; *haurient*, vertical; *embowed*, bent.

Fissure—(fi'-sure) The fourth part of the bend sinister. [See BATON.]

Fitched—[See FITCHEE.]

Fitchee—(fitsh'y) Pointed like a dagger; sharpened at the lower extremity. Fitchée is generally applied to crosses that taper from the center downward. *Fitchée at the foot* is used when the tapering begins near the bottom of the cross.

CROSS FITCHEE.

Fitchy—[See FITCHEE.]

Flamant—(flam'-ant) Flaming. burning, blazing; a torch; a firebrand.

Flanch—The segment of a circle taken

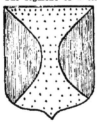

PLANCHES.

out of the two sides or flanks of the shield, the margin of which forms the cord. (Also written flasque, flanque and flaunch.)

¶ The flanch is always used in pairs—one on each side. Its diminutive is the voider. Neither is of great antiquity.

Flasque—The same as FLANCH.

Flaunch—[See FLANCH.]

Flectant — (flect'-ant) Bent serpentine fashion, like the letter S. (Essentially the same as EMBOWED.)

Flected—[See EMBOWED.]

Fleur-de-lis—(flur'-de-lee') Heraldically this is a flower, and stands at the head of the flowers of heraldry. Its origin is unknown, one "authority" claiming that it was brought down from heaven by an angel for the arms of France. It is also said to mean the flower of Louis *(Fleur de Louis)*, and was certainly used by Louis VII. It is undoubtedly the "flower of the lily."

FLEUR-DE-LIS.

Originally the royal banner of France was *semé of lis* (completely covered with fleur-de-lis); but from the time of Charles VI it has consisted of three golden fleur-de-lis on a blue field.

The fleur-de-lis did not at first meet with much favor in England, and did not become popular, in fact, until its assumption by Edward III. The French quartering in the English royal arms was abolished by George IV on his accession.

When used as a difference the fleur-de-lis represents the sixth son.

Fleurette—[See FLEURY.]

Fleury—(flu'ry) A bearing adorned with fleur-de-lis, trefoils, etc. (Also written flory, floretty, flury and fleurettée.)

FLEURY CROSS—*(Cross Fleury.)* A cross adorned with fleur-de-lis, trefolls, etc. A cross whose ends terminate in flowers. (Also called a Flourished Cross.)

Flexed—Bent, as an arm or limb. [EMBOWED.]

Floretty—The same as FLEURY.

Flory—The same as FLEURY.

Flotant—(flo'-tant) Flying or streaming in the air, as a flag flying to the breezes. When applied to a bird it is the same as VOLANT.

FLOTANT.

Flourished—[See FLEURY.]

Foldage—(fold-ige) Applied to leaves having several foldings and turnings, one from the other.

Formee—(for-may') A cross having the arms expanding toward the ends and flat at the outer edges. It differs from the cross patée in that the extremities of the formée reach the edge of the field.

Fountain—A bearing resembling the roundel. It is a disk divided by six lines wavy, tinctured argent and azure, to represent water.

Fourchee—(foor'-shay) Applied to a cross

CROSS FOURCHEE.

having the ends forked as branches, and with the ends of the branches terminating abruptly as if cut off.

Fracted—(fract'-ed) Having a part displaced, as a *chevron fracted.*

FRACTED.

Fraise—A strawberry leaf.

Free—A term applied to a horse when represented in a field.

Fret—A bearing composed of bars crossed and interlaced, representing a trellis. This was originally borne fretty. Usually composed of eight pieces. When the joints are nailed it is *clouee.*

FRET.

Fretted—Applied to charges interlaced

FRETTED.

with each other.

Fretten—The same as FRETTED.

Fretty—Applied to a bordure of eight, ten or more pieces, each reaching the extremity of the shield, and interlaced after the manner of the fret.

¶ The fret of eight parts was originally blazoned as fretty. For instance, Maltravers bore "Sable, fretty or." This later became "Sable, a fret or."

Fructed—(fruct'-ed) Bearing fruit. Applied to a tree or plant when so represented.

Funeral escutcheon — [See HATCHMENT.]

Furiosant—(fur-i-os'-ant) An epithet applied to a bull or other animal when represented as in a rage or fury. (Also called Rangant.)

Furnished—Said of a horse when borne bridled, saddled and completely caparisoned.

Fusil—(fu'-sil) An elongated lozenge. The word comes from the French *fusean*=a spindle, and the bearing is supposed to represent a distaff charged with yarn.

FUSIL.

"Fusils must be made long, and small in the middle. In the ancient coat of Montague [Montacute?], 'Argent, three fusils in fesse gules.' "—*Peacham*.

It has been said the Perceys derived their fusils from their lordship of Spindleton.

· G.

Gamb—The whole foreleg of a lion or other beast. If couped or erased near the middle joint is is called a paw.

Gambe—[See GAMB.]

Garb—A sheaf of wheat. This was a popular bearing, especially in Cheshire. Sometimes it is banded of a different color.

¶ When the garb is used to designate any other grain this must be specified.

Gardant—Applied to a beast represented full-faced, or looking at the spectator, whether the animal be rampant, passant or otherwise. A beast of the chase—such as the hart, stag or hind—when depicted in this attitude is described as *at gaze*.

Garnished—(gar'-nished) Applied to any charge provided with an ornament.

Garter—The same as BENDLET.

GARTER KING-AT-ARMS—The principal king-at-arms in England, by whom arms are granted and conferred under the authority of the Earl Marshal. The office was created by Henry V, in 1420.

ORDER OF THE GARTER—This is the most illustrious order of British knighthood. It was instituted at Windsor by Edward III in 1348. It consists of the sovereign and 25 companions, of whom the Prince of Wales is always one. In more recent times foreign princes have been admitted. The knights place the initials "K. G." after their names, which take precedence of all other titles except those of royalty.

Gauntlet—Originally a glove of leather, covered with plate metal to correspond with the other parts of the armor. It was at first worn without separate fingers.

Gaze—[See AT GAZE.]

Gemel—(gem'-el) Parallel bars. [BAR.]

GEMEL.

Gemelled—Supplied with bars gemel; placed between barrulets. [BARRULET.] [BARS GEMEL.]

Genuant—(jen'-u-ant) Kneeling.

Gerb—[See GARB.]

Gerbe—The French word sometimes used for GARB.

Gerfalcon—[See FALCON.]

Gobonated—(go'-bo-nat-ed) Applied to a bordure, bend, etc., divided into equal

GOBONATED.

parts forming squares, gobbets. (Called also goboné or gobony. [Essentially the same as COMPONY.]

Gobone—[See GOBONATED.]

Gobony—[See GOBONATED.]

Gold—This metal in heraldry is known as OR.

Golden balls—The three golden balls now universally seen as the pawnbrokers' sign were taken from the arms of Lombardy, Lombards having been the first bankers and money lenders in London.

Golden Fleece—*Order of the Golden Fleece.*—An order of knighthood instituted by Philip the Good, Duke of Burgundy. It now belongs to both Spain and Austria.

Gonfalon—(gon'-fa-lon) A banner fixed in a frame made to turn like a ship's vane; with streamers or tails, generally three.

Gore—A charge consisting of two curved lines—one from sinister chief point, the other from base middle point, meeting in an acute angle at the fesse point.

GORE.

Gorged—An animal or bird is said to be gorged when represented with a crown or something similar around its neck. It is then blazoned as "gorged with a crown," etc.

Goshawk—A bird often used in falconry, and sometimes seen as a charge. Ridley of Blaydon bore three goshawks argent.

Gradient—(gra'-di-ent) Applied to a tortoise represented as walking.

Grady—Steps or degrees, or one battlement upon another. (Also called battled-embattled and embattled grady.)

Gray—A badger.

Green—This color in heraldry is known as VERT.

Griece—A step; one of the steps upon which crosses are sometimes placed.

Griffon—A fabulous beast, generally drawn with the body, legs and tail of a lion, the

GRIFFON.

head of a cock or an eagle, a pair of wings and long, sharp claws. When represented on his hind legs he is segreant.

GRIFFON - MALE — A griffon without wings and having large ears.

Grittie—Said of a field when composed equally of metal and color.

Gryphon—[See GRIFFON.]

Guardant—[See GARDANT.]

Guelphic Order — (guel'-fick) An order of knighthood instituted for Hanover on August 12, 1815, by George IV of England, while still Prince Regent.

Gule—To color red; to give the color of gules to.

Gules—(guelz) Red. This color on engraved escutcheons is represented by vertical lines.

> "The showery arch
> With listed colors gay—or, azure, gules—
> Delights and puzzles the beholder's eye."
> —*J. Philips: Cider, ii.*

Gusset—An abatement; a mark of disgrace. It somewhat resembles a gusset, and is formed by a line drawn from either dexter or sinister chief point one-third across the shield, thence descending perpendicularly to the base. When

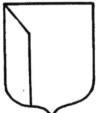

GUSSET.

on the dexter side of the escutcheon it is an abatement for adultery; when on the sinister, for drunkenness. In this connection it is scarcely necessary to say that the gusset has been rarely used. (Sometimes called a gore.)

Gutte—A drop. It is pear shaped, with a tail like a tear on funeral drapery, or like a Rupert's drop. [See also GUTTEE.]

Guttee—(gut'-tée) A shield sprinkled with guttes, or drops. Like the roundel, their name changes with the color, as follows: Or, guttée d'or; gules, guttée de sang;

argent, guttée de l'eau; sable, guttée de poix; azure, guttée de larmes; vert, guttée d'huile.

GUTTEE.

Gutty—[See GUTTEE.]

Guze—A roundel tinctured sanguine, representing an eyeball. [See also ROUNDEL.]

Gyron—(gi'-ron) A subordinary, consisting of two straight lines, drawn from any given part of the field, meeting in an acute angle in the fesse point. It is a

GYRON.

Spanish ordinary, and is supposed to come from the word *giron*, a gusse.. The gyron, which is an old bearing, is seldom used singly.

Gyronny—(gi'-ron-ny) A field divided

GYRONNY.

into gyrons, generally eig . sections. When more than eight, the number must be specified. For example: Bassing-bourne—"Gyronny of 12, or and azure."

H.

Habited—Used to describe a man when borne clothed.

Hand—The human hand plays its most prominent part in heraldry as the device of Ulster and the badge of baronets.

DEXTER HAND—The right.
SINISTER HAND—The left.

Harbored—Applied to the hart, stag, etc., when lying down. The same as couchant in beasts of prey.)

Harrington knot — Another name for the fret.

Harp—The harp is the emblem of Ireland. Its origin as the badge of Erin is obscure, but probably alludes to the instrument of Brian Boroimhe.

Harpy—The heraldic Harpy is a vulture with the head and breast of a woman.

Hart—The Hart, like the stag, is an old bearing, though not of the earliest. John Trie, son and heir of Alicia de Hertley, bore "a hart's head caboched."

Hatchment — A black panel, lozenge-shaped or square, but hung corner-wise, on which the arms of a deceased person

HATCHMENT.

are displayed ; usually hung on the walls of his or her house.

The rules governing the arrangement of the hatchment are: For a bachelor, his entire achievement on a black ground. For a single woman, her arms are placed upon a lozenge, bordered with knotted ribbons, also on a black ground. For a married man (as seen in the illustration), his arms impale those of his wife, unless she be an heiress, when they are placed on an escutcheon of pretense, the crest and other appendages added, the dexter half of the ground being black and the sinister white. For a wife, the same as for a husband, except the sinister half is black and the dexter white. For a widower, the same as for a married man, except the whole ground is black. For a widow, the husband's arms are given with her own, but upon a lozenge. In case there have been two wives or two husbands, the ground is divided into three parts per pale, the background of the survivor being white. When the deceased is a military or naval officer, colors and military or naval emblems are sometimes placed behind the arms.

"His obscure funeral:
No trophy, sword or hatchment o'er his bones,"
—*Shakespeare.*

Hatchment is the same as achievement. The word is a corruption of atchment, a shortened form of atchievement (achievement).

"By pulling down several atchievements (commonly called hatchments)."
—*Wood: Fasti Oxon.*

Haurient—(hâu'-ri-ent) Applied to a fish when borne palewise, or upright, as if putting its head out of the water to draw or suck in air.

Hausse—(hos'-say) [French.] The same as ENHANCED.

Hawk's lure—[See LURE.]

Heart—The human heart is sometimes borne. A case in point is the arms of the Douglas family in allusion to the mission of James Lord Douglas to the Holy Land with the heart of Robert Bruce. Douglas: "Argent, a man's heart gules, ensigned by a royal crown proper, on a chief azure two mullets of the first."

Hedgehog—Also known in heraldry as the herisson and the ericus. The family of Heriz bore "Azure, three hedgehogs or. The Maxwells bear the hedgehog for the lordship of Herris.

Helm—That part of a coat of arms which bears the crest.

Helmet—The helmet is borne above the shield and beneath the crest. Like the coronet, it denotes the rank of the wearer. Those used by English heralds are: (1) For sovereigns and princes of the blood, borne full-face, with six bars, all of gold; (2) for the nobility, of steel, with five bars of gold, shown somewhat in profile; (3) for baronets and knights, of steel, full-faced and open; (4) for an esquire or gentleman, of steel, with the visor closed, and represented in profile.

There is a further distinction made by some heraldic writers, being a silver helmet, in profile, with gold ornament, and four silver bars, for the lesser nobility, or those ranking below a marquis.

The various distinctions of the helmet are supposed to have been introduced after the Restoration.

Herald—An officer whose duties, among other things, consist of deciding on the proper badges or coat, armor of the nobility; to grant, record and blazon arms; record genealogies, etc. The three principal English heralds are called Kings-of-Arms (or king-at-arms). The principal herald of Scotland is called Lyon King-of-Arms; of Ireland, Ulster King-of-arms. The Lancaster herald is inspector of regimental colors.

Heraldic—(her-al'-dic) Of or pertaining to heralds or heraldry.

Heraldical—Heraldic.

Heraldically—In a heraldic manner; according to the rules of heraldry.

Heraldry—The art or science of blazoning or describing in proper terms coats of arms. It treats also of the history and meaning of armorial bearings, rules governing their use and transmission, and their connection with titular rank, family dignities and genealogies.

Heralds' College — [See COLLEGE OF ARMS.]

Heraldship—The office or dignity of a herald.

Heurt—[See HURT.]

Herisson—(her'-is-son) A hedgehog.

Heron—The heron is found in early coats of arms, being one of the few birds entitled to this distinction. The family of Heron of Chipchase and Ford, according to the roll of Henry III, bore "Gules, three herons argent."

Herring—This fish is seen in the roll of Edward II.

Hirondelle—A swallow.

Honor point— The point immediately above the center of the shield, dividing the upper portion into two equal parts.

Hood—The blinding cap on the head of a hawk (in falconry) to make him sit quietly on his perch.

Hooded—Applied to a hawk or other bird of prey when borne with a hood over its head.

Horned—Applied to animals represented with horns of a different color from the animal itself, or from the proper color of the horns. For instance, a bull with red horns would be described as *horned gules.*

Horse—The horse does not appear in early examples of heraldry, although the winged horse is seen as the badge of the Order of the Temple. A bay horse is known as a bayard, while the gray horse is a liard. When the horse is displayed caparisoned; when in the field, he is free. In harness he is said to be barded and

Horseshoe—Sometimes used as a bearing, one of the earliest examples being that of William de Ferrars, sixth earl of Derby. (Also called fer de cheval.)

Humet—[See HUMETTEE.]

Humettee—(hu-met'-tay) Said of an or-

HUMETTEE.

dinary when cut off, or couped, so that its extremities do not reach the sides of the shield.

Hunting horn—A bearing representing the bugle used in the chase.

Hurst—A charge representing a small group of trees, generally borne upon a mount or base.

Hurt—A roundel tinctured azure ; a blue ring. Some claim that it represents a wound or hurt, while others say it is a representation of the hurtleberry. [See also ROUNDEL.]

Hurty—Sown with hurts ; a field covered with hurts, without regard to number.

I.

Icicle—(i'sik-kl) A charge resembling a drop ; the same as the guttée except that it is reversed.

Illegitimacy—The *Marks of Illegitimacy* are varied, and in early examples are scarcely to be distinguished from marks of difference. The earliest known instance in English heraldry is the six lioncels borne by William Longspee, derived from his father, Henry II. Sir John Lovell le Bastard (in the roll of Edward II) bore Lovell, with a label azure. The cognizance of the Black Prince, the three ostrich plumes, became a part of the arms of his natural son, Sir Roger Clarendon. Arthur Viscount Lisle, son of Edward IV, placed a baton over his father's arms. In some cases a baton sinister was used, and sometimes it was a border. The descendants of Charles II use the whole arms with a baton sinister or border ; those of William IV the baton. With the house of Bourbon the baton distinguished the cadets, while the baton sinister marked the illegitimates.

Impale—(im-pale') To join two coats of arms palewise. (Also written empale.)

Impalement—The marshaling or arranging of two coats of arms on one shield, divided palewise, or by a vertical line. When a husband impales his arms with those of his wife, his generally occupy the dexter side, while the wife's take the sinister. This was not always the case,

however. In the impaled shield of John of Gaunt his wife, daughter of Peter of Castile and Leon, occupies the dexter ; and the same is true of William Dalziel.

IMPALEMENT.

Bishops, deans, heads of colleges, etc., sometimes impale their own arms with those of their office.

(Also written empalement.)

Impresa—(im-pree'să) [Italian.] A device, a motto ; an impress.

In—

IN BAR—[See under *Bar.*]

IN BEND—[See under *Bend.*]

IN CHIEF—[See under *Chief.*]

IN ORLE—[See under *Orle.*]

Incensant—(in-sen'sant) Applied to the boar when borne in a furious or angry position.

INCENSANT.

Incensed—(-sen'sd) A term applied to the eyes of any wild creature when represented with fire issuing from them.

Inclave—(-klave') A form resembling dovetail joints. This is applied to the lines of division on the borders of ordinaries.

Increscent—A term denoting the crescent when represented with its horns toward the dexter side of the shield.

Inde—(in'-dey) A name sometimes given to azure in ancient blazonry. The only reason or excuse for the use of the word seems to be that azure represents sapphire, and India was the principal source of supply for those gems.

Indented—Notched like the teeth of a saw. Applied to partition lines, as well as to some of the ordinaries. It differs from the dancette in that the notches in indented are smaller and apply only to the outer edge, whereas dancette affects the whole ordinary.

INDENTED.

Indentee — (-dent'ée) [French.] Having indents, not joined to each other, but set apart.

Indentilley—(-dent'-il-ley) An ordinary having long indents, somewhat resembling piles conjoined.

Indorse—[See ENDORSE.]

Indorsed—[See ENDORSED.]

Inescutcheon — (-es-kuch'-un) A small

INESCUTCHEON.

escutcheon, or shield, borne within and upon the greater shield. When voided it

becomes an orle. It is smaller than the escutcheon of pretense. The inescutcheon can be seen in some of the earliest coats.

Infamed——Applied to a lion or other beast which has lost its tail.

Inflamed—Applied to anything represented as burning or in flames. ·[FLAMANT.]

INFLAMED.

Interchangeably posed—Said of bearings placed across each other, as three fishes the head of each appearing between the tail of the other ; three swords with hilts in like position ; three arrows, etc.

INTERCHANGEABLY POSED.

Interfretted — Linked together ; inter-

INTERFRETTED.

laced. Said of any charges or bearings linked together, as interlaced crescents, interlaced keys, etc.

Interlaced—The same as INTERFRETTED.

Inveckee—(-veck'ey) A word sometimes employed by heraldic writers to describe double arching.

Invected—(-vek'-ted) The opposite of engrailed. Having a border or outline with the points turning inward toward the ordinary and the convexity toward the field.

Invertant—The same as INVERTED.

Inverted—In a contrary direction ; turned the wrong way, as a pair of wings with the points downward.

Invexed—Arched or enarched.

Islay—One of the heralds of the Lord Lyon's Court, Scotland.

Iron Cross—*Order of the Iron Cross—A* Prussian order of knighthood, instituted in 1813.

Issuant—(ish'-u-ant) Issuing or coming out of. A charge represented as issuing

ISSUANT.

from another charge. When an animal is represented as issuant only the upper half is depicted.

J.

Jamb—[See GAMB.]

Jelloped—(jel'-lopd) Said of the comb and gills of the cock when of a different color from the body. (Also written jowlopped. [WATTLED.]

Jessant — (jes'-sant) Springing up or shooting forth, as a plant. Also applied to an animal, in the same sense as issuant.

Jessant-de-lis — Used to describe the head of a leopard having a fleur-de-lis passing through it.

Jessed—Having jesses on. (Said of a hawk).

¶ The jesse, used in falconry, was a short strap of leather or silk with which hawks were tied by the leg and on which the leash was attached.

Jowlopped—[See JELLOPED.]

K.

King-of-Arms—An officer who has jurisdiction over armory, etc. There are three in England—Garter, the principal ; Clarenceaux, whose jurisdiction extends south of the Trent ; and Norry, who officiates north of that river. The King-of-Arms for Scotland is called Lyon ; and for Ireland, Ulster. The office of King-of-Arms is one of great antiquity.

Kintyr—One of the pursuivants of the Lord Lyon's Court, Scotland.

Knight—One who holds the dignity of knighthood, conferred by the sovereign, entitling the holder to the title of Sir prefixed to his name. Unlike a baronet, however, the dignity is not hereditary. The wife of a knight is legally entitled to the designation of Dame, but by common consent is addressed as Lady.

Formerly a candidate for knighthood had to go through certain ceremonies or religious rites, preparing himself by fasting and prayer and by watching his arms alone all night in a chapel.

KNIGHT BACHELOR—The lowest order of knighthood ; also the oldest.

KNIGHT BANNERET.—A knightly order next below the Garter. [See *Banneret.*]

KNIGHT ERRANT—A knight who wandered about the country in quest of adventures for the purpose of displaying his prowess.

L.

Label—A bearing closely resembling the strap with pendants which from the saddle crossed the horse's chest. It is the oldest mark of difference, but sometimes borne as a charge. As a difference it was used generally by the princes of the royal house. The number of points did not necessarily mean anything, although the label of three points was supposed to represent the heir during the lifetime of his father; five points, during the lifetime of his grandfather: seven points, while the great-grandfather still lived, etc. According to the modern system, the elder son of an elder son places a label upon a label.

LABEL.

Lace d'amour—(leese dǎ'moor) A cord of running knots surrounding the arms of widows and unmarried women. *(Universal Dict.)*

Lambrequin—(lam'-ber-kin) The point of a label.

☞A mantle is sometimes referred to as a lambrequin. (In this connection see MANTLE.)

Lampasse—(lam-pas-see') [French.] The same as LANGUED.

Lancaster—One of the six heralds of the College of Arms.

Lance—Shakespeare's father was granted arms as follows: "Or, on a bend sable a lance of the field."

Langued—(langd) Tongued: having the tongue visible. Applied to the tongue of a bird or beast when of a different tincture from that of the body.

Lattice—A bordure formed of perpendicular and horizontal bars, interlaced or otherwise.

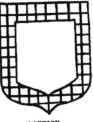

LATTICE.

Laver—A green vegetation, a bunch of which is held in the mouth by the liver on the arms of Liverpool.

Leaf—The leaves common to heraldry are the strawberry, hazel, oak and elm.

Legged—The same as MEMBERED.

Leopard—The real spotted leopard is neither an early nor a common bearing. Sometimes called a pard.

Leopard—The title of one of the heralds under Henry V.

Leo-parde—"A lion as a leopard." The early heralds seem to have gotten the lion confused with the leopard, and when describing him in any attitude except passant he was *leo-parde*.

Leonced—[See LIONCED.]

Liard—A gray horse.

Limbeck—[See DISTILLATORY.]

Lion—The Lion is the most popular beast in heraldry. He appears in the arms of Great Britain, Denmark, Spain, Holland, Bohemia, Saxony and numerous lesser countries. As early as 1127 Henry I used the lion as an ornament on a shield. Of the 918 bannerets of Edward II, 225 bore lions. The early English heralds seem to have confused the lion with the leopard. While never drawn spotted as the real leopard, he was described in most attitudes as leo-parde, or a lion as a leopard.

The lion is drawn in about 30 attitudes, but it is seldom he is seen in other than rampant or passant.

LION'S WHELP—The same as *lioncelle.*

LION OF ENGLAND—In allusion to the lions on the arms of Great Britain. In English heraldry a lion passant gardant or is generally blazoned as "a lion of England."

Lionced—(li'unst) A bearing adorned with lions' heads, as, for instance, a cross with its ends terminating in lions' heads.

Lioncel—[See LIONCELLE.]

Lioncelle—(li'un-sel) A small lion. Specifically, the lioncelle is one of several borne in the same arms.

Liver—A fabulous bird, after which Liverpool is supposed to have derived its name. It resembles the cormorant. The arms of Liverpool are blazoned: "Argent, a liver sable, billed and legged gules, holding in his bill a bunch of laver vert."

LIVER.

"The liver was a foolish invention to account for the name [of Liverpool]. There was the 'pool,' which accounted for the last syllable, and there was the bird on the seal or shield, which, in the absence of other information, was supposed to indicate the prefix. A stuffed bird has from time immemorial been preserved in the Town Hall, supposed to be a specimen of the genus *liver.* It is, in reality, an immature cormorant, which has not attained its final dark plumage." —*Sir J. A. Picton, in Notes and Queries,* May 3, 1884.

Lodged—Applied to the buck, hart, hind, etc., when represented lying down.

¶ The same attitude of the lion or similar beast is couchant.

Lord Lyon—[See LYON KING-OF-ARMS.]

Lowered—Applied to ordinaries abated from their common position.

Lozenge—(loz'enj) 1. A diamond-shaped bearing, usually with its upper and lower angles slightly acute.

2. The form of the escutcheon upon which women place their arms. Specifically, for spinsters and widows.

¶ As the shield was used in war, it was peculiar to men, and the female had no part therein; hence an unmarried woman from earliest times placed her arms on a lozenge, perhaps in allusion to the fusil, or distaff; when married, she shares the shield of her husband.

Lozengee—[See LOZENGY.]

Lozengy—(loz'en-jy) A bearing or the field divided into lozenge-shaped compart-

LOZENGY.

ments of different tinctures, the lines being drawn in the direction of the bend and bend sinister.

Luce—A fish; a full-grown pike.

Lure—(lur) A bunch of feathers. (The lure was used in falconry to recall the hawks.)

Lymphad—(lim'-fad) A galley; an ancient vessel, having one mast. It is not uncommon in Scottish heraldry; is the feudal ensign of the lordship of Lorne, being quartered by the Dukes of Argyll, and is also borne by the Clan Campbell.

Lyon Court—The office or court of Lyon King-of-Arms; the Scottish college of arms.

Lyon King-of-Arms—A Scottish official (also called Lord Lyon) who derives his title from the lion rampant on the arms of Scotland. He has authority to inspect the arms and ensigns armorial of all noblemen and gentlemen in the kingdom; to give proper arms to those entitled to bear them; to matriculate such arms, and to fine those bearing arms which are not matriculated. He is assisted by heralds, pursuivants and messengers-at-arms.

M.

Macle—(mak'l) The same as MASCLE.

Majesty—A term used to describe an eagle crowned and holding a scepter.

Maltese cross—A cross formed of four arrow heads meeting at the points. It was the badge of the Knights of Malta, and its eight points are said to symbolize the eight beatitudes.

Man—The full human figure is a rare bearing, but can be seen occasionally. When displayed naked, he is *salvage;* when clothed, *habited.*

Manche—[See MAUNCH.]

Mantiger—(man'-ti-ger) A monster with the body of a lion or tiger and a human face, usually with a scorpion's tail and long spiral horns. (Also written Mantichor and Manticor.)

Mantle—The cloak or robe behind the shield, sufficiently large to include the entire arms. Those of sovereigns are of gold doubled with ermine, and are called pavilions.

Mantling—[See MANTLE.]

Marchmont—One of the heralds of the Lord Lyon's Court, Scotland.

Marcassin—(mar-kas'-sin) [French.] A young wild boar.

Marined—ma-reend') An animal having the lower part of the body like a fish.

Marquis—A nobleman in England, ranking next below a duke.

Mars—The name of the color gules (red) on the arms of sovereign princes.

Marshal—To dispose or arrange in order such coats of arms as have to be included in one shield.

Marshaling—The act of arranging two or more coats on one shield.

Martlet—(mart'-let) A fanciful bird somewhat resembling a swallow, but having short tufts of feathers in the place of legs. When used as a difference it denotes the fourth son.

Mascle—(mas'-kl) a lozenge-shaped bearing, perforated or voided. When used in numbers it becomes *masculy.*

MASCLE.

Masculy—(mas'-ku-ly) A field covered with mascles conjoined, resembling network.

Massacre—(mas'-sa-ker) When the antlers of a stag are attached to a fragment of the skull bone it is called a massacre.

Masoned—(ma'-sond) Applied to a field or charge which is divided with lines resembling a wall or building of stones.

Maul—A heavy wooden hammer.

Maunch—(maunsh) A bearing representing a sleeve with long hanging ends.

Membered—A term applied to a bird when its legs are of a different tincture from that of the bird itself.

Merchants' marks—Certain marks or bearings used by merchants of England. such as the block and brush (butchers' broom) of the Butchers' Company; the distillatory, of the Distillers' Company, etc. They are not to be considered strictly heraldic, but were protected by law. and are occasionally seen on merchants' tombs and in architecture.

Merlon—[See EMBATTLED.]

Metal—[For the metals of heraldry see under TINCTURE.]

Millrind—A bearing supposed to represent the iron which holds a millstone by being set into its center.

Millrynd—[See MILLRIND.]

Miter—The headdress of a bishop, sometimes used as a charge, either singly or in numbers.

MITERS.

Mitry—(mi'try) Charged with eight miters. Said of a bordure.)

Modulata—[See BOTTONY.]

Moline—[See *Cross Moline, under* CROSS.]

Moon—The moon in heraldry is always borne as a crescent, usually with the cavity upward. When the cavity is toward the dexter side of the shield, it is *increscent;* when toward sinister, *decrescent.*

Mooted—Torn up by the roots; eradicated.

Morion—A steel cap; a kind of helmet, shaped something like a hat, and having no beaver or visor.

Morne—(mor'nay) Without teeth, tongue or claws. (Said of a lion.)

Motto—A word or sentence carried on the scroll, and supposed to have some connection with the name of the bearer, the deeds of his ancestors or as setting forth some guiding principle or idea. Mottos, like arms, were sometimes punning, as *Cavendo tutus,* the motto of the Cavendishes; *Ver non semper viret,* of the Vernons. The Scotch borderers, whose chief delight in life seemed to be that of harrying their neighbors by moonlight, used stars and crescents for their arms and adopted such mottos as *Watch weel* (Halyborton) and *Reparabit cornua*

Phoebe (Scott of Harden).

The motto is the successor of the war-cry, which was common in the days when each chief tenant and baron under the crown brought into the field and led his own tenants and retainers. The royal cry of the English was "St. George for England;" the common Highland cry was "Claymore," while Seyton had "St. Bennett and Set on."

Mound—A ball or globe forming part of the regalia of a king or emperor. It is surmounted by a cross and represents sovereign authority.

Mount—The representation of a mound or hill, covered with grass, occupying the base of the shield. It is generally borne with a tree or trees on it. When depicted green it is blazoned as a *mount vert.*

MOUNT-GRECED—A mount cut in the form of steps.

MOUNT-MOUNTED—A mount with a hill upon it.

Mounted—1. Applied to a horse when depicted bearing a rider.

2. When a cross or similar bearing is placed upon steps, as a cross mounted upon greces, or degrees.

Mullet—A bearing resembling a five-pointed star. It is sometimes called a spur rowel, but it was in use long before the rowelled spur. When used as a difference it denotes the third son.

Muraille — (mu-rail'-ley) Walled; masoned and embattled.

Murrey—(mur'-ry) The same as SANGUINE.

Muschetor—(mus'-che-tor) One of the arrow-headed marks used in depicting ermine, but without the three round dots employed in blazing that fur.

Musca—(mus'-ka) The common housefly. In some coats, however, this becomes a butterfly.

Musion—A cat.

Muzzled—Having a muzzle. Said of an animal, such as a bear, borne with a muzzle.

N.

Naiant—(na'-yant) [French.] The same as NATANT.

Naissant—(nas'-sant) Rising or coming forth. Applied to any living creature represented as issuing out of a fesse or other ordinary.

Natant — (nay'-tant) Represented horizontally across the field, as if swimming toward the dexter side of the shield. Applied to any fish excepting the flying fish and shell fish.

NATANT.

Naval crown—A crown formed with the stern and square sails of ships placed alternately upon the circle or fillet.

Navel point—The point in the shield between the middle base point and the fesse point. (Also called the nombril.)

Nebule—[See NEBULY.]

Nebuly—(neb'-u-ly) 1. Composed of undulations, like the wavy edges of clouds.

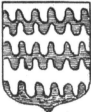

NEBULY.

2. A shield or bearing divided by such lines.

3. A wavy line of partition, or by which ordinaries and subordinaries may be bounded.

Nombril—(nom'bril) A point in the shield between the fesse point and the middle base point. (Also called the navel point.)

Norroy—The third English King-at-Arms. He has jurisdiction north of the Trent.

Nowed—(nowd) Knotted; tied in a knot, as a serpent or the tail or a lion.

NOWED.

"Ruben is conceived to bear three bars wave, Jude a lyon rampant, Dan a serpent nowed."—*Browne: Vulgar Errours.*

Nowy—(now'y) A term applied to a projection in the middle of a cross or other ordinary.

Nowyed—(now'yed) Applied to a projec-

NOWYED.

tion not in the center of a cross, but in its branches.

O.

Octofoil—A double quatrefoil; a leaf of eight points. When used as a difference it denotes the eighth son.

Office—*Arms of Office.* [See under ARMS.]

Ogress—(o'gress) A black ball or pellet. [See ROUNDEL.]

Onde—(on'dey) [French.] Wavy; curved and recurved like waves. [UNDE.]

Ondy—[See ONDE.]

Opinicus—(o-pin'-i-kus) An imaginary animal having the head and wings of a griffon or eagle, a short tail like that of a camel and the body of a lion.
The Opinicus is sometimes borne without wings.

Or—Gold. In engraving it is denoted by small dots or points spread all over the bearing or field.
"Azure, an eagle rising or, the sun
In dexter chief." —*Tennyson.*

Orange—[See ROUNDEL.]
☞The color of orange in heraldry is known as *tenné.*

Orb—A globe encircled, bearing a cross; a mound.

Ordinary—A charge or bearing of simple form. The ordinaries, or, as they are called by the majority of heraldic writers, *honorable ordinaries,* are nine in number, as follows:

Chief,	Cross,
Pale,	Saltire,
Fesse,	Pile,
Chevron,	Quarter.
Bend,	

The honorable ordinaries are said to represent the clamps or fastenings of the shield, becoming ornamental from painting or gilding. Each has one or more diminutives.

Organ rest—[See REST.]

Orle—(orl) 1. One of the subordinaries; in the form of a fillet, within the border, but some distance from it.
"His arms were augmented with an orle of lion's paws."—*Fuller: Worthies,* I, 129.
2. The wreath or chaplet surmounting or encircling the helmet of a knight and bearing the crest. (*Webster.)*

IN ORLE—Said when the charges are placed round the escutcheon, leaving the middle of the field vacant, or occupied by something else. (Said of bearings arranged on the shield in the form of an orle.)

Ormond—One of the pursuivants of the Lord Lyon's Court, Scotland.

Oundy—[See UNDY.]

Out of—Signifies rising from, as "out of a ducal coronet an eagle."

Overt—(o'vert) Applied to the wings of a bird, etc., when spread open on each side of its head, as if taking flight.

P.

Pale—One of the nine honorable ordinaries. It is a vertical line, set upright in the middle of the shield and occupying

PALE.

one-third of the field. It seldom contains more than three charges.

PARTY PER PALE—[See under *Party.*]

Palewise—In the manner of a pale or pales; divided by perpendicular lines; to divide the field palewise.
"Hath behind it palewise an abbot's crosier."
—*Wood: Fasti Oxon,* I, 12.

Pall—A figure having the form of the let-

PALL.

ter Y. It consists of half a pale issuing from the base, and conjoined in the fesse point with half a saltire from the dexter chief and sinister chief.

Pallet—(pal'-let) A diminutive of the pale, being one-fourth of its breadth. (Some writers say one-half.)

Palletted—(pal'-let-ted) Being conjoined by a pallet; as "A chevron palletted."

PALLETTED.

Palmer's staff—A branch of a palm tree carried by a palmer in token of his having been to the Holy Land.

Paly—(pale'y) A field divided into four or more equal parts by perpendicular lines of two tinctures alternating. The num-

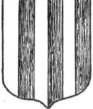

PALY.

ber should always be specified; as, "Paly of six argent and gules."

PALY BENDY—When the divisions are again cut by diagonal lines, either dexter or sinister.

Papagay—(pap'-a-gay) A popinjay. An early bird in English heraldry.

Pard—A leopard.

Parted—[See PARTY.]

Partition—One of the several divisions made in a coat when the arms of several families are borne on one shield, from intermarriage, etc. [In this connection see QUARTERING.]

PARTITION LINES—The lines by which a shield may be divided. They are closely allied to the ordinaries for which they are named. When a field is divided in the direction of an ordinary it is said to be "party per" that ordinary; as, *party per pale, party per bend*, etc. Unless otherwise specified, the partition lines are straight; they may, however, be drawn in a variety of ways, such as undy, embattled, dancetté, etc.

Party—Parted; divided. Used in reference to any division of a field or charge. When the field is divided toward an ordinary it is said to be "party per" that ordinary.

PARTY PER BEND—When the field is divided by a line running diagonally from the dexter chief to the sinister base.

PARTY PER PALE.

PARTY PER CHIEF—Divided by a horizontal line one-third the distance of the field from the top of the shield. (Party per chief is rare.)

PARTY PER CROSS—This is called *Quarterly.*

PARTY PER PALE—Divided by a perpendicular line.

PARTY PER FESSE—Divided by a horizontal line in the center of the shield.

Passant—(pas'-sant) Walking; said of any animal, except beasts of the chase, when represented as walking, with the dexter paw raised.

☞The same attitude in the case of a stag, hart, etc., would be *trippant.*

Patee—(pa'-tay') Spreading out at the extremity; applied principally to a cross. (Also written paté and pattée.)

Paternal—*Paternal Arms.* [See under ARMS.]

Patonce—(pay-tons) Applied to a cross having expanded ends, like the cross patée, each end terminating in three points.

Patriarchal cross — (pa'tri-ar'kal) A cross in which the shaft is twice crossed, the lower arms being longer than the upper.

Patronage—*Arms of Patronage.* [See under ARMS.]

Patte—[See PATEE.]

Pavilion—(pay-vil'-yun) A sort of mantling or cloak in the form of a tent investing the coat of arms of a sovereign. [MANTLING.]

Pavon—(pay'-von) A flag borne by a knight in the Middle Ages, upon which his arms were displayed. It was of triangular form, smaller than the pennon, and affixed to the upper part of his lance.

Pean—(peen) One of the furs. The ground is sable, with the spots or tufts or.

Pearl—The same as ARGENT.

Pelican—(pel'-i-kan) While this bird is occasionally seen in arms, it is more common as a crest. When represented as wounding herself, she is *vulning;* when feeding her young, *in her piety.* Pelham bore "Azure, three pelicans vulning themselves proper."

PELICAN IN HER PIETY.

PELICAN IN HER PIETY—A pelican represented in the act of wounding her breast to feed her young with her own blood. This came from a fabulous tale in natural history told in the Middle Ages, and which made the bird the adopted symbol of the Redeemer.

Pellet—(pel'-let) A black roundel. (Also called ogress and gunstone.) [See also ROUNDEL.]

Penned—(pend) Having wings. (Applied to a hawk's lure. [See LURE.]

Pennon—A small flag or streamer half the size of the guidon.

Per—By; by means of; by way of.

Perclose—(per'-kloz) The lower part of the garter with the buckle, etc. (Also called the demi-garter.)

Perculaced—(per'-ku-last) The same as LATTICE.

Peregrine falcon—[See FALCON.]

Pheon—(fee'on) A bearing representing the head of a broad arrow or javelin, with long barbs which are engrailed on the inner edge.

PHEON.

¶ The pheon was, like the modern mace, carried before royalty by a sergeant-at-arms. It became a royal mark, and is still used in Great Britain to denote crown property, being termed the Broad R, or broad arrow.

Pick—An instrument used in the chase; a spike; a pike.

Pierced—Applied to any bearing which is perforated so as to show the field under it.

Pike—A military weapon, consisting of a long, narrow lance head fixed to a pole. It was used by musketeers to repel cavalry.

Pile—One of the honorable ordinaries, having the form of a wedge, issuing from the chief, with the point ending with the lower point of the shield. When borne plain it contains one-third of the chief in breadth; when charged, two-thirds. The pile is a very early bearing. and its origin is obscure. It has no diminutives.

PILE.

Per pile—Applied to an escutcheon which is divided by lines in the form of the pile.

Plate—A roundel tinctured argent. [See also ROUNDEL.]

Plenitude—(plen'-i-tude) Fullness. When the moon is represented full it is described as "the moon in her plenitude."

Plie—The same as CLOSE.

Ploye—(plwa-ye') Bowed and bent.

Poing—(pwân) The fist; the hand closed, as distinguished from apaumé.

Point—1. One of the several parts denot-

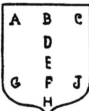

POINTS.

ing the local positions on the escutcheon of any figure or charges. The principal points are :

A.—Dexter chief,   F.—Nombril (navel).
B.—Middle chief,   G.—Dexter base.
C.—Sinister chief,   H.—Middle base.
D.—Honor, or color.   J.—Sinister base.
E.—Fesse (center).

2. A small part of the base of a shield variously marked off.

POINT IN POINT—When the base somewhat resembles the pile.

Pointed—Said of a cross when its ends are so cut; as, a *cross pointed.*

Pomey—(pom'y) A figure representing an apple; it is always of a green color. A roundel tinctured vert.

Pommee—(pom'-may') A cross having the ends terminating in single balls.

CROSS POMMEE.

Pommette—(po'-may-tay') A cross having two balls or buttons at each end.

Pommeled—Having a pommel, as a sword or dagger.

Portant—The same as PORTATE.

Portate—(por'-tat) Borne bendwise; diagonally across the escutcheon. Example: A *cross portate*=a cross lying as if carried on a person's shoulder.

Portcullis—The same as LATTICE.

Portcullis—One of the pursuivants of the College of Arms.

Pose—(po'-zay') Said of a lion, horse or other beast when represented standing still, with all four feet on the ground.

Potence—(po'-tens) A cross having ends that resemble the head of a crutch.

Potent—(po'-tent) One of the heraldic furs, composed of patches, supposed to represent crutch heads; the color is usually argent and azure alternating. If otherwise, this should be specified. Potent is a variety of vair, and in early times was often blazoned "vair-potent."

COUNTER-POTENT—A fur differing from

potent only in the arrangement of the patches. (Also written potent counter-potent. potency counter-potency and potency in point.)

CROSS POTENT—[See *potence.*]

Potented—Applied to a bearing when the outer edges are T-shaped, or formed into potents.

Powdered—The same as SEME.

Prancing—Applied to a horse represented rearing.

Prester John—A mythical descendant of Ogier the Dane. In the Middle Ages he was believed to rule as a Christian sovereign and priest in the interior of Asia.

¶ A representation of the Prester John may be seen on the arms of the See of Chichester.

Pretense—*Escutcheon of Pretense.* [See under ESCUTCHEON.]

Pretension—*Arms of Pretension.* [See under ARMS.]

Prey—*At prey* is applied to the falcon when represented feeding.

Preyant—The same as PREYING.

Preying—Applied to any beast or bird of prey when represented standing on and in a proper position for devouring its prey.

Pride—A term applied to the peacock, turkey cock and other birds which spread their tails in a circular form and drop their wings; as, "A peacock in his pride."

Prince—Heraldically speaking, the title of prince belongs to dukes, marquises and earls of Great Britain; but in ordinary usage it is restricted to members of the royal family.

PRINCE OF WALES—The official title of the heir apparent to the throne of England.

PRINCES OF THE BLOOD—The younger sons of a sovereign.

PRINCE ROYAL—The eldest son of a sovereign.

Proper—Represented in its natural color. Said of charges; as, "a lion proper."

Purfle—(pur'-f'l) To ornament with a bordure of ermines, etc.

Purfled — (pur'-feld) Trimmed or garnished. Applied to the studs and rims of armor, being gold; as, "a leg in armor purfled or.

Purflew—(pur'-flu) A border of fur shaped exactly like vair. When of one row only, it is called purflewed; when of two, counter-purflewed; when of three, vair.

Purple—This color in heraldry is known as PURPURE.

Purpure—(pur'-pure) Purple. It is represented in engraving by diagonal lines declining from the right top of the shield to the left base (from sinister chief to dexter base).

Pursuivant—(pur'-swe-vănt) An official in the English College of Arms. There are four pursuivants—Rouge Croix, Blue Mantle, Rouge Dragon and Portcullis. There were formerly six pursuivants attached to the court of Lyon King-of-Arms, in Scotland—Unicorn, Carrick, Bute, Kintyre. Ormond and Dingwall. The last three have been abolished.

Pye—The popinjay; the woodpecker.

Q.

Quarter—One of the ordinaries (also called *franc-quartier*), occupying one-fourth of the shield, and usually placed in dexter chief. If placed in sinister chief, this must be specified. The diminutive of the quarter is the canton, of two-thirds its area.

QUARTER.

Quarter—To add to other arms on a

shield; to bear as an appendage to the hereditary arms.

2. To be quartered.

GRAND QUARTER—The same as *sub-quarter.*

SUB-QUARTER—A quarter set aside in quartering arms out of the regular order for the royal arms or for an heiress when her quarterings are not broken.

Quartered—A term sometimes applied to the cross when voided in the center; as "a cross quartered."

Quartering—The arrangement of two or more coats of arms on one shield to form one bearing, as, for instance, the royal arms of England, where those of the several countries are conjoined; when a man inherits from both father and mother the right to bear arms; when an alliance of one family with the heiress of another is to be perpetuated.

☞When only two coats are quartered on one shield, as in the case of marriage, the first and fourth quarters display the arms of the husband; the second and third, those of the wife.

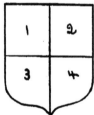

QUARTERS.
1—First, or dexter chief, quarter.
2—Second, or sinister chief, quarter.
3—Third, or dexter base, quarter.
4—Fourth, or sinister base, quarter.

☞In quartering arms, the shield may be divided into as many squares as necessary, and the first coat (that of the bearer) may be repeated or not to make up an even number.

Quarterly—Placed in quarters; an escutcheon divided into quarters.

Quatrefoil—(kwa'-ter-foil) A four-leaved grass. This is frequently seen in heraldry.

Quarter-pierced—Said of a cross when the central square is removed; as, a cross quarter-pierced.

Queue—(ku) The tail of a beast.

QUEUE FURCHEE—The same as *double queued.*

Queued—(ku'd) Tailed; having a tail of a different tincture.

DOUBLE QUEUED—Having a double tail, as a lion. Sometimes the tails are placed saltirewise.

Quilled—(kwild) This term is used in describing a feather when the quill differs in color from the rest.

Quinque vulnera—(kwin'-kwe vul'-ne-ra) The five wounds of the crucifixion. This is an ecclesiastical bearing.

R.

Radiant—Edged with rays or beams; giving off rays; as, "A sun radiant."

Ragged—[See RAGULY.]

Ragulated—[See RAGULY.]

Raguled—[See RAGULY.]

Raguly—(ray-gul'y) Notched or jagged in an irregular diagonal manner. Said of a line or bearing having such an edge.

CROSS RAGULY.

Rampant—(ramp'-ant) Said of a beast of prey, as a lion, rising with fore paws in the air, as if attacking. The right fore leg and right hind leg should be raised higher than the left. Unless otherwise specified, the animal faces dexter.

COUNTER-RAMPANT—Said of two animals rampant in opposite directions.

(Sometimes used to denote a beast rampant toward sinister.)

RAMPANT GARDANT—The same as rampant, but with the animal looking full-faced.

RAMPANT PASSANT—Said of an animal when walking with the dexter fore paw raised somewhat higher tnan the mere passant position.

RAMPANT REGARDENT—In a rampant position and looking behind.

RAMPANT SEJANT—A beast in a sitting posture, with the fore legs raised.

Rangant—The same as FURIOSANT.

Range—(ran'-zhay) [French.] Arranged in order.

Raping—Applied to any ravenous beast represented devouring its prey.

Ravissant—(rav'-is-sant) [French.] In a half-raised position, as if about to spring on prey. (Said of the wolf and such beasts when in the attitude saliant.)

Ray—A ray of the sun. [See SUN.]

Rayonee—[See RADIANT.]

Rayonnant—[See RADIANT.]

Rayonned—[See RADIANT.]

Razed—The same as ERASED.

Rebate—A diminution or abatement of a bearing, as when the point of a weapon is broken off, or a part of a cross cut off.

Rebated—Having the points cut short or broken off.

Rebending—Bent first one way and then the other, like the letter S. [RECURV-ANT.]

Rebus—A pictorial suggestion on a coat of arms of the name of the owner; a bearing or bearings containing an allusion to the owner's name. Thus the Arches family bore three arches; the Dobell family, a doe between three bells. [See also *Allusive Arms*, under ARMS.]

Recercelee—[See *Cross Recercelee*, under CROSS.]

Reclinant—(re-klin'-ant) The same as DECLINANT.

Recouped—The same as COUPED.

Rectangled—When the line of length is apparently cut off in its straightness by another straight line, which at the intersection makes a right angle, it is then termed *rectangled*.

Recursant — (re-kur'-sant) Said of an eagle displayed, with the back toward the spectator.

RECURSANT.

RECURSANT VOLANT IN PALE—An eagle represented flying upward, with its back toward the spectator.

Recurvant—(re-kurv'-ant) Curved and recurved, like the letter S.

Red—This color in heraldry is known as GULES.

Reflected—Curved or turned round, as the chain or line from the collar of an animal thrown over his back.

Regardant—Said' of an animal whose face is turned toward the tail in an attitude of vigilance; looking backward.

Reined—Said of a horse when the reins are of a different color from the animal. [BITTED.]

Removed—[See FRACTED.]

Rempli—(ran-plee') [French.] Said of the chief when filled with any other color or metal, leaving only a border of the first tincture visible.

Renverse—(ren-vers') Reversed; turned contrary to the natural position; with the head down; set upside down; as, "A chevron renverse."

Repassant—(re-pass'-ant) A lion or other animal passant, facing the sinister side of the shield.

¶ Some writers use this term to describe beasts passant, one facing dexter and the other sinister. In this connection see *counter-passant,* under COUNTER.

Reremouse—(rere'-mouse) a bat.

Reserved—Contrary to the usual way or position. *(Univers. Dict.)*

Resignant—(rez'-ig-nant) [French] Concealed. Said of a lion when his tail cannot be seen.

Respectant—(re-spekt'-ant) Two animals borne face to face.

☞Rampant beasts of prey so borne are said to be combatant.

Rest—A bearing the origin and meaning of which have been disputed. By some it is said to represent a spear rest, and perhaps this is correct. By others it is taken for a musical instrument of some kind. Hence it is sometimes called an organ rest.

REST.

Retorted—Said of serpents when wreathed one in another, or fretted in the form of a knot.

Retracted—Applied to charges when one is shorter than the other.

Reversed—A coat of arms or escutcheon turned upside down. This was done by way of ignominy, as in the case of a traitor.

Revertant—Bent and rebent.

Reverted—Bent or curved twice in opposite directions, like the letter S; revertant.

Ribbon—A diminutive of the bend, being one-eighth its size, and often used as a difference. When couped or cut short it becomes a baton.

Richmond—One of the heralds of the College of Arms.

Ringed—Provided with a ring or rings. (Said of the falcon.)

¶ In the days of falconry it was the custom to slip over the claws of the young falcon a silver ring, which could not afterward be removed.

Rising—A bird represented as if in the act of taking flight; rising from the ground.

Rizon—(riz'on) The grain of oats.

Roach—A fish.

Rompee—[See ROMPU.]

Rompu—(rom'pu) Fracted; broken; parted asunder, as a chevron, bend, etc.

Rose—The Rose, which is popular in English heraldry, is generally borne singly and full-faced, with five petals, barbs and seeds.

Ross—One of the heralds of the Lord Lyon's Court, Scotland.

Rothesay—One of the heralds of the Lord Lyon's Court, Scotland.

Rondle—[See ROUNDEL.]

Rook—A rook in heraldry is the bird of that name common in Great Britain. It resembles the crow, but is smaller. When the piece in chess known as a rook is borne it is blazoned a chess-rook. They are sometimes seen on the same arms, as in the case of Rook of Kent: "Argent, on a chevron engrailed between three rooks sable, as many chess-rooks of the first."

Rouge Croix—(roozh' kroi') One of the pursuivants in the College of Arms.

Rouge Dragon—(roozh' drag'-on) One of the pursuivants in the College of Arms.

Roundel—A subordinary in the form of a circle. If of a metal it is a simple disk; if of a color, it is convex, half a globe. It takes its name from its color, unless in case of counter-changes, which follow the tinctures of the field, or when the roundel is of fur or of equal tinctures, as "a roundel ermine," "a roundel checky or and azure." Otherwise roun-

ROUNDELS.

dels have distinguishing names, according to their tinctures. They are seldom borne singly, and are as follows:

When or they are Bezants.
When argent they are Plates.
When gules they are Torteaux.
When azure they are Hurts.
When vert they are Pommes.
When purpure they are Golpes.
When sable they are Pellets.
When tenne they are Oranges.
When sanguine they are Guzes.

The pellet is sometimes called a gunstone or ogress.

FALSE ROUNDEL—This was a name given in early lists for the annulet. Thus the arms of Vipont were blazoned "Gules, six false roundels or."

Rousant—(rouz'-ant) Rising. Said of a bird in the attitude of rising; preparing to take flight. Sometimes this term is applied to a bird in profile, as a swan with wings addorsed.

Rowel—[See MULLET.]

Royal arms—[See *Arms Royal*, under ARMS.]

Rudented—The same as CABLED.

Rustre—(rus'-ter) A lozenge pierced round in the center, and exposing the field through it.

S.

Sable—The tincture black. In engraving it is represented by perpendicular and horizontal lines crossed.

St. Andrew's cross—A cross made in the form of the letter X. [See SALTIRE.]

St. Patrick—The title of one of the pursuivants of the Office of Arms, Ireland. There are three pursuivants bearing this title, designated as Nos. 1, 2 and 3.

Saliant—(sa'-li-ant) Leaping; springing. Applied to the lion or other beast represented in a leaping posture—his fore feet in dexter chief and his hind feet in sinister base.

Salient—[See SALIANT.]

Saltant—(sal'-tant) Springing forward; in a leaping position. Applied especially to the squirrel, weasel, rat; also applied to the cat, greyhound and monkey.

Saltier—[See SALTIRE.]

Saltire—(sal'-teer) One of the honorable ordinaries. It is made in the form of a St. Andrew's cross, or the letter X. Its breadth should be one-third of the field. The saltire is popular in Scottish heraldry.

SALTIRE.

Saltirewise—In the manner of a saltire; when the shield is divided by two lines drawn in the direction of a bend and a bend sinister and crossed at the center. Long-shaped charges, such as swords, oars, batons, etc., placed in the direction of the saltire are said to be borne saltirewise.

Salvage—Said of a man when borne nude. Thus, "Three salvage men ambulant."

Sanglier—(sang'-li-er) [French.] A wild boar.

Sanguine—(san'-gwin) A dark red color. It is represented in engraving by diagonal lines crossing each other.

Sapphire—The same as AZURE.

Saturn — Black: representing sable in blazoning the arms of sovereign princes.

Scallop—The same as ESCALLOP.

Scarf—A small ecclesiastical banner hanging down from the top of a crosier.

Scarp—(skarp) A diminutive of the bend sinister. occupying the same position as that bearing, but being only half its breadth. It is supposed to represent an officer's shoulder belt or scarf.

Scrape—[See SCARP.]

Scroll—The ribbon-like appendage to a crest or escutcheon, on which the motto is inscribed.

Scutcheon—[See ESCUTCHEON.]

Sea lion—A monster consisting of the upper part of a lion combined with the tail of a fish.

Seruse—The same as TORTEAU.

Seeded—Represented with seeds of a different tincture, such as the rose, lily, etc., when it is said to be *seeded of* that color.

Segreant—(se'-gre'-ant) Said of a griffon when depicted standing on its hind legs, with the wings elevated and addorsed.

Sejant—In a sitting posture. Applied to the lion, cat, etc.

SEJANT ADDORSED—Said of two animals sitting back to back.

SEJANT AFFRONTE—Full-faced, sitting. with the fore paws extended sideways.

SEJANT RAMPANT—[See *rampant sejant.*]

Sejeant—[See SEJANT.]

Seme—(sem'ay) A field or charge powdered or sprinkled with small charges, such as stars, crosses, etc. (Sometimes called powdered.)

Shack bolt—A' fetter, such as might be put on the wrists or ankles of prisoners.

Shackle bolt—The same as SHACK BOLT.

Shake fork—A bearing somewhat resembling the pall in form, but the ends, which have points like the pile, do not touch the edges of the shield.

SHAKE FORK.

Sheldrake — A water fowl somewhat larger than the ordinary duck. It has been said that this bird was introduced into English heraldry to accommodate Sheldon, Lord Mayor of London in 1676. He bore "Sable, a fesse between three sheldrakes argent."

Shield—The escutcheon or field on which are placed the bearings of coats of arms. There are various forms, mostly taken from the shapes in vogue when shields were used in warfare. Maiden ladies and widows have no shield, but place their arms on a lozenge. [LOZENGE.] [ESCUTCHEON.]
[For different forms of shield see Illustrated Supplement.]

Shoveller—A river duck. It has a broad bill and beautifully variegated feathers.

Sinister—(sin'-is-ter) The left side of the shield—the side opposite the right hand of the spectator. Applied to the escutcheon. as the *sinister chief point, sinister base point*, etc.

Sinople—(sin'-o-pl) The Continental term for vert (green).

Slashed—A term used to describe the opening or gashings in a sleeve when the puffing is of a different tincture. It is then *slashed of* such a tincture.

Slipped—Applied to a flower or branch depicted as torn from the stalk.

Snowdown—One of the heralds of the Lord Lyon's Court, Scotland

Soarant—A word used by some modern heraldic writers' as a synonym of VO-LANT.

Sol—A term implying or (gold) in blazoning the arms of sovereign princes.

☞Using the planets in blazoning the arms of emperors, kings and princes arose in the sixteenth century through the foolish fancy of some heraldic writers, as did the use of precious stones for the arms of peers.

Somerset—One of the heralds of the College of Arms.

Soustenu—(soos'-ten-u) A chief apparently supported by a small part of the escutcheon beneath it of a different tincture from the chief itself, and reaching, as the chief does, from side to side ; being, so to speak, a small part of the chief of another color, and supporting the real chief.

Soutenu—[See SOUSTENU.]

Spade iron—The iron part, or shoeing, of a spade.

Spancelled—(span'-seld) Said of a horse that has the fore and hind feet fettered by means of fetterlocks fastened to the ends of a stick.

Spayade—(spa'-yade) A stag in his third year.

Spear—The spear was an ancient instrument of war and hunting, and was introduced into heraldry under various forms. Generally called a lance.

Spear head—The metal point of the spear : a common bearing among the Welsh.

Speckled—Spotted ; speckled over with another tincture.

Spectant—(spek'-tant) The attitude of an animal looking upward with nose bendwise. Also applied to an animal at gaze, or looking forward. (Sometimes called *in full aspect.)*

Speller—A branch shooting out from the first part of a buck's horn at the top.

Sperver—A tent.

Splendor—Glory ; brilliance. Said of the sun when represented with a human face and environed with rays. It is then a *Sun in splendor.*

Spread eagle—An eagle having the wings and legs extended on both sides. [DISPLAYED.]

Springing—Leaping. Applied to beasts of the chase in the same sense as saliant to beasts of prey. Also applied to fish when placed in bend.

Spur rowel—The mullet is often called a spur rowel, which it is supposed to represent. However, the mullet was in use long before the rowelled spur.

Stainand — (stain'-and) Applied to the sanguine and tenné when used in the figures called abatements=marks of disgrace.

Standard—A flag or ensign. The ancient military standard consisted of a symbol carried on a pole, like the Roman eagle. In mediæval times the standard, instead of being square like the banner, was elongated, but much larger, becoming narrow and rounded at the end, which was slit, unless the standard belonged to a prince of the blood royal. The standard, which ranged in size from eleven yards for an emperor to four yards for a baron, was usually divided into three portions—one containing the arms of the knight, another for his cognizance or badge, and the other for his crest—these being divided by bands, on which was inscribed his war cry or motto, the whole being fringed with his livery or family colors.

"Knights bannerets are made in the field, with the ceremonie of cutting of the point of his standard, and making it as it were a banner."—*Smith: Commonwealth, bk. i, chap. xviii.*

The English royal standard of today is properly a banner, being square, with its entire field covered solely by the national arms.

Star—An estoile. It differs from the mullet in that it usually has six rays wavy, and is seldom pierced. When more than six points are displayed, the number must be specified. Usually, when more than six, the points alternate straight and wavy.

Statant — (stay'-tant) Standing. (The same as posé.)

Stone bill—A wedge.

Stopped—[See EMBATTLED.]

Subordinary—A bearing not so common and of less importance than the ordinary, or honorable ordinary. According to one writer, any ordinary occupying less than one-fifth of the field is deemed a subordinary. Again, different writers place different bearings among the subordinaries. The following list, however, many recognized authorities agree on:

Bordure,	Fusil,
Flanch,	Mascle,
Fret,	Rustre,
Inescutcheon,	Roundel,
Gyron,	Gutte,
Lozenge,	Billet,
Orle,	Checky,
Tressure,	Voider.

Subvertant — (sub-vert'-ant) Reversed; turned upside. down; contrary to the natural position or usual way of bearing.

Subverted—[See SUBVERTANT.]

Succeedant—Succeeding or following one another.

Succession—*Arms of Succession.* The same as *Feudal Arms,* which see, under ARMS.

Sun—The Sun is seen in heraldry occasionally. When represented as giving light, it is blazoned *a sun radiant;* when depicted with a human face, it is *a sun in splendor,* or a sun in his splendor. Louis XIV used it as his cognizance. Jean de la Hay bore "Argent, a sun in his splendor gules." Ralph de la Hay differenced this coat by bearing only a ray of the sun. John de Fontibus, Bishop of Ely, bore the sun, moon and seven stars.

☞When the ray only is used, it generally issues from dexter chief.

Sunburst—A flag having a sun in splendor on a green field. This is said to have been the flag of the pagan Irish. It is frequently alluded to in Irish national poetry.

"On the front ranks before,
Dathi the sunburst bore."
—*Fate of King Dathi.*

Supercharge—(-charj) 1. To place one figure upon another.

2. *As a noun:* One charge placed upon another charge; as, a rose upon a fesse.

Supported—Applied to a bearing that has another under it by way of support; as, a chief supported.

Supporter—A figure on each side of a shield, apparently supporting it. They may be men, beasts or birds—sometimes real, sometimes fabulous, as the lion and unicorn in the arms of Great Britain.

The origin of the supporters is unknown. Some writers have set forth that they originated in the ceremonial bearing of the knightly shield to tournaments and jousts by squires. It is probable, however, that they arose from the ornaments of the seal engraver and became heraldic from the practice of quartering.

Supporters are now borne by all peers of Great Britain, Knights of the Garter, Knights Grand Cross of the Bath, Nova Scotia baronets and chiefs of Scottish clans, and are also borne by many municipalities and the principal mercantile companies of London.

Sur-ancree—A cross with double anchor flukes at each end.

SUR-ANCREE CROSS.

Surcharged—One charge placed upon or within another.

Surgiant—The same as ROUSANT or RISING.

Surmounted—Partly covered. Said of an ordinary when it has another charge of a different tincture laid over it.

☞When it is an animal which has a charge laid over it, the term used is debruised.

Surtout—(sur'-too) [French.] A shield of pretense; an inescutcheon placed upon a shield of arms. The arms of William III were so disposed of.

Suspectant—Looking upward. (The same as SPECTANT.

Swallow—This bird, which is also known as the hirondelle, is an early bearing. One of the best known of the early examples is the arms of the Arundells of Wardour, who bore "Sable, six swallows argent."

Swan—The swan was the cognizance of the Bohuns. Sometimes it is borne whole, sometimes only the head, like the arms of the Guests. When gorged with a ducal coronet having a gold chain attached to it, it is called a cygnet-royal.

Swift—The dolphin.

Sweep—The balista or engine anciently used for casting stones into fortresses.

Sword—The sword of heraldry is two-handed.

T.

Tabard—Originally a light vestment worn over the armor embroidered with the arms of the wearer. The tabard is now worn only by heralds and pursuivants-at-arms, and is embroidered with the arms of the sovereign.

Talbot—A dog. Specifically a hound whose race is nearly, if not quite, extinct. His color was pure white, with large head, broad muzzle and long ears. Talbot is the family name of the Earls of Shrewsbury, who had a talbot for a badge and two talbots for supporters.

Talent—The same as BEZANT.

Targant—[See TORQUED.]

Tau—The cross of St. Anthony, also called the Cross Tau. It derives its name from its resemblance to the Greek letter tau. This cross is somewhat similar to the cross potent.

Tawney—[See TENNE.]

Tawny—[See TENNE.]

Tegulated—(teg'-u-la'ted) Composed of small plates as of horn or metal, overlapping. (Used in ancient armor.)

Templar—A member of the order called Templars, Knights Templar, Knights of the Temple, etc. It was founded in 1118 or 1119 by nine Christian knights, the original object of the organization being to maintain free passage for the pilgrims visiting the Holy Land. Baldwin II King of Jerusalem gave them part of his palace, and they kept their arms in the Temple, hence their name of Templars.

Tenant—Held; holding.

Tenanted—Tailled or let into another thing; one bearing worked into another bearing; having something let in; as, a cross tenanted==having rings let into its extremities.

Tenne—(ten'-nay) A tincture of a bright brown, which is considered to represent orange color. This color is almost unknown in English heraldry. In engraving it is represented by diagonal lines from sinister to dexter, traversed by horizontal ones—a compound of purpure and azure.

Tent—The representation of a tent used as a bearing. [See also PAVILION.]

Tergant—(ter'-gant) Showing the back part; as, an eagle tergant displayed. [In this connection compare RECURSANT.]

Terras—The representation of ground at the bottom of the base of the shield, generally tinctured vert.

Teutonic cross—A name sometimes given to the cross potent from the fact of its

TEUTONIC CROSS.

having been the original badge assigned by Emperor Henry VI to the knights of the Teutonic Order.

Teutonic Order—A religious military order of knights established near the end of the twelfth century somewhat like the Templars and Hospitallers, being composed in the main of Teutonic crusaders. It attained high power, but declined in the fifteenth century, and was finally abolished by Napoleon in 1809.

Thane—A title of dignity or honor among the Anglo-Saxons. There were two orders—the king's thanes, or those who attended at his court and held lands immediately from him, and ordinary thanes, or lords of the manor. After the Norman conquest thanes and barons were classed together, the title falling into disuse in the reign of Henry II.

Thistle—The *Order of the Thistle*, a Scottish order or knighthood, was instituted by James VII (James II of England) in 1687. It fell into abeyance during the reign of William and Mary, but was revived by Queen Anne in 1703.

Thunderbolt—The thunderbolt is represented in heraldry by a twisted bar in pale, inflamed at the ends, surmounting two jagged darts in saltire, between two wings expanded, and usually has streams of fire issuing from the center.

THUNDERBOLT.

Tiara—The triple crown worn by the popes of Rome.

Tierce — (ter-say') Divided into three equal parts of three different tinctures. (Said of the field when so divided.)

Tiercelet—(ters'-let) A falcon.

Tiger—The heraldic tiger has the body of a wolf, the tail of a lion and is studded with tufts of hair. It is not an early bearing, nor is it often seen.

Timber—1. A row of ermine in a nobleman's coat.

2. The helmet, miter, coronet, etc., when placed over the arms in a complete achievement.

3. *(As a verb)* To surmount or decorate the coat of arms.

"A purple plume timbers his stately crest."
                                —*Sylvester.*

Timbre—(tim'-ber) [French.] The crest which in an achievement is shown on the top of a helmet.

Tincture—(tink'-tur) The name given to the colors, metals and furs used in heraldry. The tinctures may be classed as follows:

METALS.

Or (gold, yellow)   Argent (silver, white)

COLORS.

Azure (blue)   Sable (black)
Gules (red)   Vert (green)
Purpure (purple)

Of later introduction are sanguine (dark red) and tenne (orange). They are, however, almost unknown in English heraldry.

FURS.

Ermine   Vair-en-point
Ermines   Counter-vair
Erminois   Pean
Erminites   Potent
Vair   Counter-potent

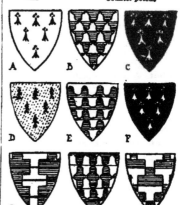

FURS.

Ermine (A)—Represents the skin of

that little animal. and is white powdered with black spots.

Ermines (C)—A black field. with white spots.

Erminois (D)—The field is gold and the spots sable.

Erminites—The same as ermine, except that the two lateral hairs of each spot are red.

Vair (B)—Similar in shape to small escutcheons, the wings representing the fore legs and the point the tail. The skins are arranged alternately white and blue. If other colors are used they must be specified.

Vair-en-point—A variety of vair, the point of one escutcheon being placed opposite to the base of the one below.

Counter-vair (H)—Another variety of vair, those of the same color being placed base to base and point to point. (Vair was originally drawn bell-shaped, as seen in E.)

Pean (F)—The reverse of erminois, being golden spots on a black field.

Potent (I)—The skins are T-shaped, resembling somewhat a gallows or a crutch head. It is akin to vair, and is sometimes blazoned "vair-potent."

Counter-potent (G)—A variety of potent, being placed point to point. (Also called potent counter-potent.)

The practice of representing the several colors by lines and marks, which dates from the sixteenth century, is as follows:

Argent—A plain white surface.

Or—Small dots.

Azure—Horizontal lines.

Gules—Vertical lines.

Purpure—Diagonal lines from sinister to dexter.

Vert—Diagonal lines from dexter to sinister.

Sable—Vertical and horizontal lines.

Sanguine—Diagonal lines from right to left and left to right (in saltire).

Tenné—Diagonal lines from sinister to dexter and horizontal (a compound of purpure and azure).

A foolish practice arose during the sixteenth century of blazoning the arms of princes and peers by precious stones and planets. The system was as follows:

Or—topaz, Sol.

Argent—pearl, Luna.

Azure—sapphire, Jupiter.

Gules—ruby, Mars.

Purpure—amethyst, Mercury.

Sable—diamond, Saturn.

Vert—emerald, Venus.

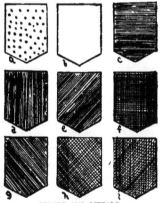

COLORS AND METALS.

a, Or ; *b*, Argent ; *c*, Azure ; *d*, Gules ; *e*, Purpure ; *f*, Sable ; *g*, Vert ; *h*, Sanguine ; *i*, Tenné.

Tirret—(tir'-ret) A manacle.

Topaz—(to'-paz) The name given to the metal or when borne by peers.

Torce—The same as WREATH.

Torgant—[See TORQUED.]

Torqued — (torkt) Twisted ; wreathed ; bent. This term is used to describe a dolphin haurient, twisted into a form nearly resembling the letter S.

TORQUED.

Torteau—(tor'to) .A roundel tinctured gules. (Plural, torteaux.) [See also ROUNDEL.]

Tourne—(toor'nay') [French.] The same as CONTOURNE or REGARDANT.

Transfixed—Pierced by an arrow or similar weapon. Said of an animal.

Transfluent—(-flu'ent) Passing or flowing through the arches of a bridge. (Said of water when so represented.)

Transmuted — The same as COUNTERCHANGED.

Transpierced—[TRANSFIXED.]

Transposed—(-pozd') Reversed; changed to a position the opposite of the proper or usual position; as, a pile transposed.

Traversed—(trav'-ersd) Turned to the sinister side of the shield.

Treflee—(tray'-flay') Having a three-lobed extremity or extremities, as a cross. [CROSS BOTTONY.] Ordinaries, such as the bend, are sometimes borne tréfléée—that is, with trefoils issuing from the side.

Trefoil—(tree'-foil) A charge representing the three-leaved clover. Like the rose, it is generally, though not always, borne without a stalk.

Trefoiled—The same as TREFLEE.

Treille—(trel) Cross-barred work; lattice work. It differs from fretty in that the pieces do not interlace under and over, but cross athwart each other, being nailed at the joints. (Also called trellis.)

TREILLE.

Trellis—The same as TREILLE.

Tressure—(tresh'-ur) A kind of border or hem, being, in fact, a diminutive of the orle, of which it is one-half its breadth. It passes around the field, following the shape and form of the escutcheon, whatever shape it may be; usually borne double. Being used in the royal arms of Scotland, it is naturally popular in Scottish heraldry.

TRESSURE FLEURY—A tressure ornamented with fleur-de-lis on one side, with their ends inward.

TRESSURE FLEURY-COUNTER-FLEURY—A double tressure ornamented with fleur-de-lis on both sides, the flowers being reversed alternately. In the arms of Scotland, as in nearly all examples, the flower is divided by the border.

Tressured—Provided with a tressure; arranged in the form or occupying the place of a tressure.
> "The tressured fleur-de-lis he claims
> To wreath his shield, since royal James."
> —*Sir Walter Scott.*

Trian—(tri'an) The aspect of an animal when neither affronté nor gardant, but midway between those positions.

Triarchee—(tri-ar'shee) Formed of three arches; having three arches.

Trick—To draw in outline, as with a pen; to delineate without color, as coats of arms.
> "They forget they are in the statute, the rascles; they are blazoned there; there they are tricked, they and their pedigrees."—*Ben Johnson: Poetaster, i, 1.*

Tricorporal—(-kor'-po-ral) Three bodies conjoined to one head, as a lion; the bodies of three beasts represented issuing from the dexter, sinister and base points, and conjoined to one head in the center of the shield.

Tricorporate—The same as TRICORPORAL.

Trien—(tri'-en) Three. The word is made use of by some heralds in the phrase a *trien of fish*=three fish.

Triparted—Parted into three pieces; having three parts or pieces. This can be applied to the field or to the ordinaries and charges; as, triparted in pale, a cross triparted, etc.

Triple crown—The crown or tiara worn by the popes of Rome.

Triple pile—A truncated pile, ending in three projections.

Triple plume—The device of the Prince of Wales.

Trippant—(trip'-pant) Having the right forefoot lifted, the other three remaining on the ground, as if trotting. This term is applied to beasts of chase, as a buck, hart, etc., and is the same as passant, which is applied to beasts of prey.

COUNTER-TRIPPANT—Two animals borne trippant contrary ways, as if passing each other.

Tripping—The same as TRIPPANT.

Triton—(tri'-ton) A variety of sea shell.

Tronconee demembre — (tron-kon-ay' de-mem'-bray) [French.] Separated; applied to a bearing, such as a cross, cut in pieces and separated, but still retaining its original form.

TRONCONEE DEMEMBRE.

Truncheon—(trun'shun) A baton, or staff of authority.

The truncheon is the official badge of the Earl Marshal. It is a golden rod, tipped with black enamel, being blazoned at one end with the arms of the sovereign, and at the other with those of the Earl.

Trunked—(trunkt) 1. When the trunk of a tree is of a tincture different from the branches it is said to be *trunked of* such a tincture.

2. Applied to a tree which has been shorn of its branches and separated from its roots.

Tuberated—Knotted or swelled out.

Turnstile—A revolving frame in a footpath to prevent the passage of horses or cattle, but admitting that of a person. A representation of this is occasionally seen as a bearing.

Tusked—(tuskt) Having tusks of a different tincture from that of the body. Said of an elephant, boar, etc. Example: If a boar was white with red tusks, he would be blazoned "A boar argent, tusked gules."

Twyfoil—Having only two leaves.

Tyrwhit—The lapwing.

U.

Ulster badge—The badge of the province of Ulster, Ireland — a sinister hand, couped at the wrist apaumé gules. ("A bloody hand"). This was assigned by James I as the badge to the baronets who were to colonize Ulster. It is now borne by all baronets of England and Ireland.

ULSTER BADGE.

Ulster King-at-Arms — The chief heraldic officer for Ireland. The office was created by Edward VI in 1552.

Unde—(un'-dy) Waving or wavy. This term is applied to ordinaries or lines of division. (Also written undy; the French call it ondé.)

Undy—The same as UNDE.

Unescutcheoned—(-es-kuch'-und) Without an escutcheon; without a coat of arms.

"To this loved cemetery, here to lodge,
With unescutcheoned privacy interred."
—*Wordsworth.*

Ungued—[See UNGULED.]

Unguled—Having hoofs of a tincture different from that of the body. (Said of a horse, stag, etc.

Unicorn—(u'ni-korn) A fabulous animal, with the head, neck and body of a horse, a beard like that of a goat, the legs of a buck, the tail of a lion, and a long tapering horn, spirally twisted, in the middle of the forehead. The royal arms of Scotland had unicorns for supporters until the union with England, in 1603. The sinister supporter of the present arms of Great Britain is, "A unicorn argent, armed, crined and unguled or, gorged with a coronet of crosses patée and fleur-de-lis, with a chain affixed passing between the fore legs and reflected over the back of the last."

Unicorn—One of the pursuivants of the Lord Lyon's Court, Scotland.

Unifoil—A plant with only one leaf.

Urdee—(ur'-dey) Pointed. The cross urdée is an ordinary cross with the ends drawn to a sharp point instead of being cut straight.

CROSS URDEE.

Urinant—(ur'-in-ant) The opposite of haurient. This term is applied to the dolphin or other fish when represented with the head downward and the tail erect.

Urvant—(ur'-vant) Turned or bowed upward.

Urved—[See URVANT.]

V.

Vair—One of the furs of heraldry, composed of a number of pieces cut to resemble little shields, and arranged alternately argent and azure. When of different tinctures they must be specified; as, "vairy argent and vert." Other varieties of vair are: *vair-en-point*, where the point of one shield, or skin, is placed opposite to the base of the one below; *counter-vair*, where those of the same color are placed base to base and point to point. (Vair was originally drawn bell-shaped.)

VAIR-POTENT—The same as *potent*.

Vaire—(val'ry) The same as VAIRY.

Vairy—Checkered or charged with vair.

Vambraced—(vam'-braced) Armed with a vambrace.
¶ The vambrace was the portion of armor which covered the arm from the elbow to the wrist.

Variated—[See VARRIATED.]

Varment—(var'-met) The escallop when represented without the ears.

Varriated—(var'-ri-ated) A bearing cut in the form of vair; as, a bend varriated on the outsides.

Varries—Separate pieces of vair, the form resembling a small shield or escutcheon.

Varrys—[See VARRIES.]

Varvelled — When the leather thongs which tie on the bells to the legs of hawks are borne flotant, with rings at the ends, the bearing is then termed jessed, belled and varvelled.

Velloped—(vel'-opd) Having gills of a different tincture from that of the bird itself. Applied to a cock when so borne. [WATTLED.]

Venus—When blazoning arms of princes by planets, as some foolish heralds have done, Venus represents the tincture vert.

Verdoy—(ver'-doi) Applied to a bordure charged with leaves, fruits, flowers, etc.; as, a bordure verdoy of trefolls.

Vergette—(ver'-jet) A small pale: a pallet; also, a shield divided with pallets.

Versant—(ver'-sant) Erected or elevated.

Vert—The tincture green. In engraving it is expressed by diagonal lines from dexter chief to sinister base. In fanciful blazonry vert is also known as emerald and Venus.

Vertant—(ver'-tant) Formed like the letter S. [The same as FLECTED and REFLECTED.]

Vigilant—Applied to a cat when represented as on the lookout for prey.

Virole—(vi-role') The hoop, ring or mouthpiece of a bugle or hunting horn.

Viroled—(vi-rold') Furnished with a virole or viroles. Said of a bugle or horn when borne with rings of a different tincture from the bugle itself.

Viscount—(vi'-kount) In Great Britain, the fourth rank of nobility, being above a baron and below an earl.

Visitation—An official visit made by a king-at-arms to take note of all armorial bearings within his jurisdiction. These visitations were made about every thirty years. A provincial king-at-arms, either personally or by deputy, would visit the principal town of his province or county and summon all the gentry to come forward and record their respective pedigrees and show title to their armorial bearings, all of which data would later be recorded at the College of Heralds. The first regular commission of visitation was issued by Henry VIII in 1528-9, but there had been visitations of one form or another as early as 1412. The last visitation took place early in the reign of James II.

Visor—That part of a helmet in old armor which protected the face, and which could be lifted up or down at pleasure.

Visored—With the visor down, or closed.

Voided—Having the inner part cut away, leaving a narrow border, with the tinc-

CROSS VOIDED.

ture of the field showing in the vacant space; a bearing in outline only.

Voider—One of the subordinaries, being a diminutive of the flanch. It resembles the flanch, but is smaller and has a flatter curve.

¶ In defensive armor the voider was a gusset piece, of plate or mail, which was used to cover an unprotected space at the elbow or knee joints.

Vol—A pair of wings; two wings conjoined and displayed in base.

Volant—Represented as flying, or having the wings spread as in flight. Applied to a bird; as, an eagle volant.

Vorant—(vor'-ant) Devouring. Applied to an animal depicted devouring another.

Vulned—(vulnd) Wounded. Applied to an animal or bird depicted as wounded and bleeding; as, a leopard vulned.

Vulning—Wounding; in the act of wounding. This term is applied more particularly to the pelican, which, when shown in profile, is generally represented as wounding her breast. [PELICAN IN HER PIETY.]

W.

Water budget—(buj'et) A bearing which represents the ancient water budget, or

WATER BUDGET.

bucket, consisting of two leather vessels connected by a stick or yoke and carried over the shoulder. They were used by soldiers for carrrying water on long marches, and were also utilized by water carriers to convey water from the conduits to the houses of the citizens.

The water budget is an early and frequent bearing in English heraldry.

Watery—A term sometimes used to express UNDE.

Wattle—The fleshy lobe that grows under the throat of a domestic fowl.

Wattled and combed—When the gills and comb are of a different tincture from that of the body. (Said of the cock.)

Waved—The same as UNDE.

Wavy—The same as UNDE.

Welt—A narrow border to an ordinary or charge.

Whelk—The ordinary sea shell.

Whelk's shell—The same as WHELK.

White—This color in heraldry is known as ARGENT.

White Cross Knight—A Hospitaller. These knights wore a white cross to distinguish them from the Knights Templar, who wore a red cross.

White spur—A kind of esquire. *(Cowel.)*

Wildcat—[See CAT.]

Windsor—The name of one of the six heralds in the College of Arms.

Winged—Depicted as having wings; or having wings of a different tincture from the body.

Winged lion—This was the symbol of St. Mark, and was adopted as the heraldic device of the Venetian republic, when St. Theodore was supplanted as the patron saint of Venice by St. Mark. The bearing may be blazoned: "Azure, a winged lion sejant gardant, with a glory or ; in his fore paws an open book, thereon 'Pax tibi, Marc, Evangelista Meus,' over the dexter page a sword erect, all proper."

Wiver—[See WYVERN.]

Wivern—[See WYVERN.]

Wood—The same as HURST.

Wreath—The roll or chaplet above the shield, supporting the crest. It is supposed to represent a twist of two silken cords, one tinctured like the principal metal, the other like the principal color, in the arms. Wreaths may also be circular, but the straight wreath is by far the more common.

Wyvern—An imaginary animal—a two-

WYVERN.

legged dragon, the body passing off into a long tail barbed at the end and generally borne nowed or knotted.

Y.

York—The name of one of the six heralds in the College of Arms.

AN ILLUSTRATED

· SUPPLEMENT.

ABASED.
(Page 1.)

AFFRONTEE.
(Page 2.)

WINGS ABASED.
(Page 1.)

ALLERION
(Page 3.)

ADDORSED.
(Page 2.)

ANCHORED.
(See Anchored Cross, page 3.)

ANCHORED CROSS.
(Page 3.)

ASHEN KEYS.
(Page 7.)

ANNULET.
(Page 4.)

ATTIRED.
(Page 7.)

ARGENT.
(Page 4.)

AVELLANE CROSS.
(Page 7.)

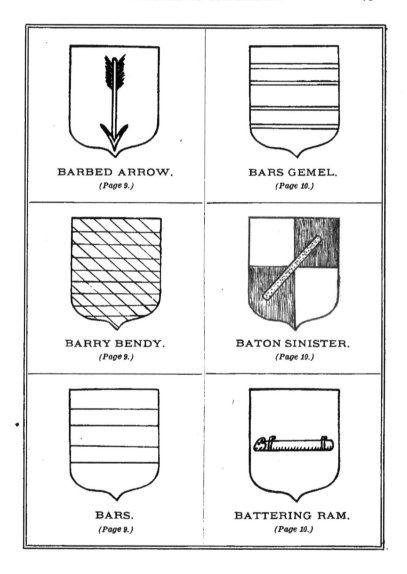

BARBED ARROW.
(Page 9.)

BARS GEMEL.
(Page 10.)

BARRY BENDY.
(Page 9.)

BATON SINISTER.
(Page 10.)

BARS.
(Page 9.)

BATTERING RAM.
(Page 10.)

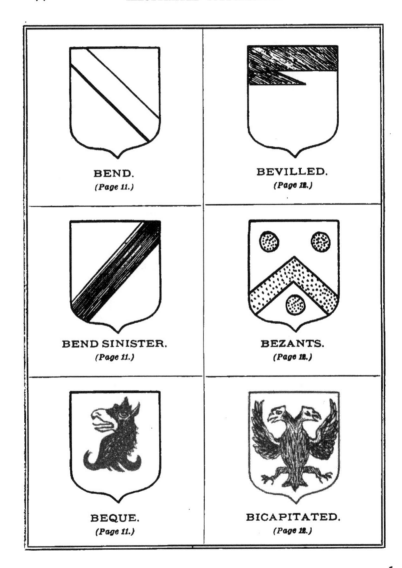

BEND.
(Page 11.)

BEVILLED.
(Page 12.)

BEND SINISTER.
(Page 11.)

BEZANTS.
(Page 12.)

BEQUE.
(Page 11.)

BICAPITATED.
(Page 12.)

BICORPORATE.
(Page 12.)

BORDURE.
(Page 14.)

BILLET.
(Page 12.)

BOTTONY.
(Page 14.)

BIRD-BOLT.
(Page 13.)

BRACED.
(Page 14.)

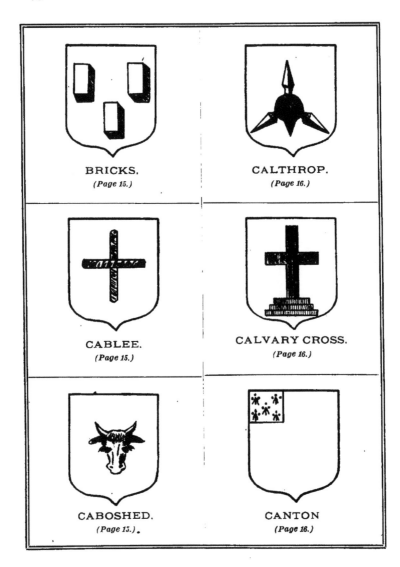

BRICKS.
(Page 15.)

CALTHROP.
(Page 16.)

CABLEE.
(Page 15.)

CALVARY CROSS.
(Page 16.)

CABOSHED.
(Page 15.)

CANTON
(Page 16.)

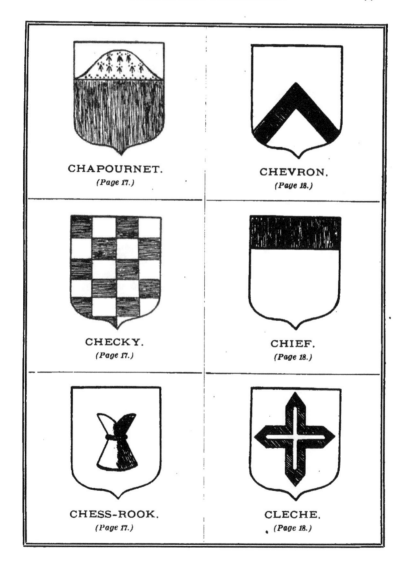

CHAPOURNET.
(Page 17.)

CHEVRON.
(Page 18.)

CHECKY.
(Page 17.)

CHIEF.
(Page 18.)

CHESS-ROOK.
(Page 17.)

CLECHE.
(Page 18.)

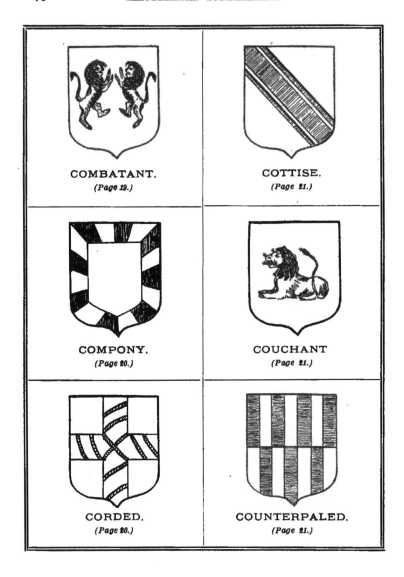

COMBATANT.
(Page 19.)

COTTISE.
(Page 21.)

COMPONY.
(Page 20.)

COUCHANT
(Page 21.)

CORDED.
(Page 20.)

COUNTERPALED.
(Page 21.)

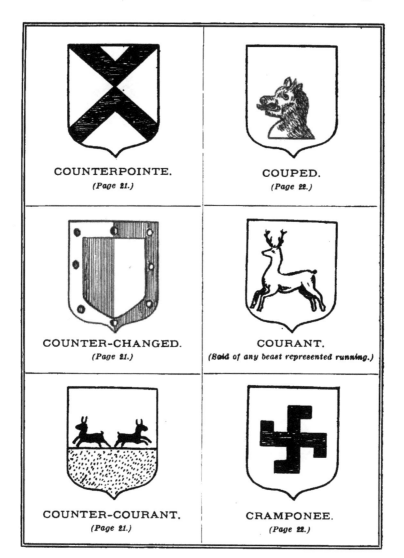

COUNTERPOINTE.
(Page 21.)

COUPED.
(Page 22.)

COUNTER-CHANGED.
(Page 21.)

COURANT.
(Said of any beast represented running.)

COUNTER-COURANT.
(Page 21.)

CRAMPONEE.
(Page 22.)

CRESCENT.
(Page 22.)

CREST.
(Page 22.)

DECRESCENT.
(Page 26.)

CROSS CROSSLET.
(Page 23.)

INCRESCENT.
(Page 42.)

CYGNET ROYAL.
(Page 25.)

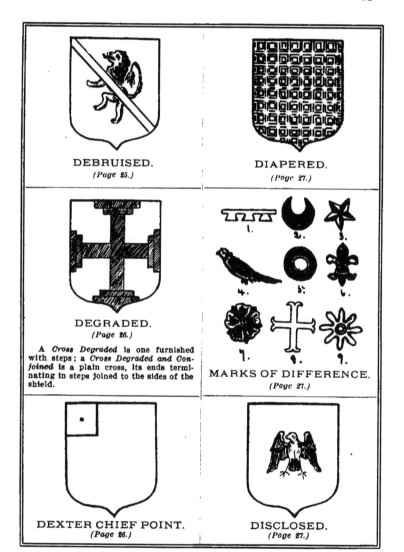

DEBRUISED.
(Page 25.)

DIAPERED.
(Page 27.)

DEGRADED.
(Page 26.)

A *Cross Degraded* is one furnished with steps; a *Cross Degraded and Conjoined* is a plain cross, its ends terminating in steps joined to the sides of the shield.

MARKS OF DIFFERENCE.
(Page 27.)

DEXTER CHIEF POINT.
(Page 26.)

DISCLOSED.
(Page 27.)

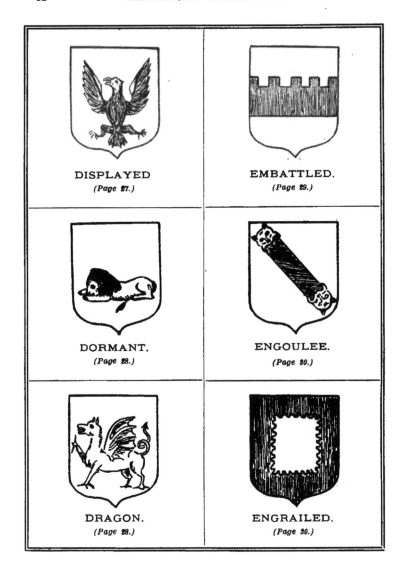

DISPLAYED
(Page 27.)

EMBATTLED.
(Page 29.)

DORMANT.
(Page 28.)

ENGOULEE.
(Page 30.)

DRAGON.
(Page 28.)

ENGRAILED.
(Page 30.)

ENHANCED.
(Page 81.)

ESTOILE.
(Page 32.)

ERMINE.
(Page 31.)

FESSE.
(Page 33.)

ESCALLOPEE.
(Page 32.)

FETTERLOCK.
(Page 33.)

FITCHEE.
(Page 34.)

FLOTANT.
(Page 35.)

FLANCHES.
(Page 34.)

FOURCHEE.
(Page 35.)

FLEUR-DE-LIS.
(Page 34.)

FRACTED.
(Page 35.)

FRET.
(Page 35.)

FUSILS CONJOINED.
(Page 36.)

FRETTED.
(Page 35.)

GARDANT.
(Page 36.)

FUSIL.
(Page 36.)

AT GAZE.
(Page 7.)

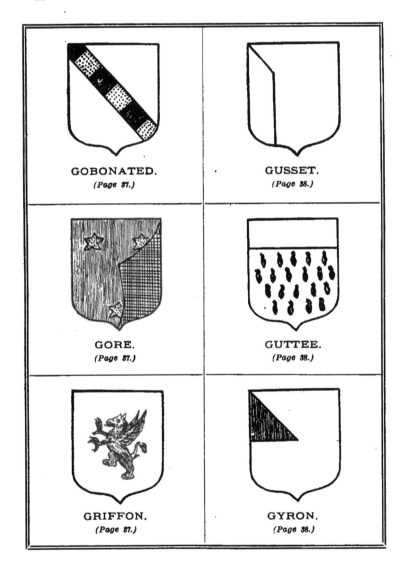

GOBONATED.
(Page 87.)

GUSSET.
(Page 88.)

GORE.
(Page 87.)

GUTTEE.
(Page 88.)

GRIFFON.
(Page 87.)

GYRON.
(Page 88.)

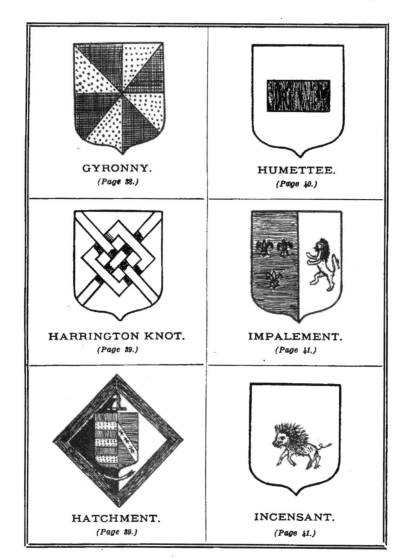

GYRONNY.
(Page 38.)

HUMETTEE.
(Page 40.)

HARRINGTON KNOT.
(Page 39.)

IMPALEMENT.
(Page 41.)

HATCHMENT.
(Page 39.)

INCENSANT.
(Page 41.)

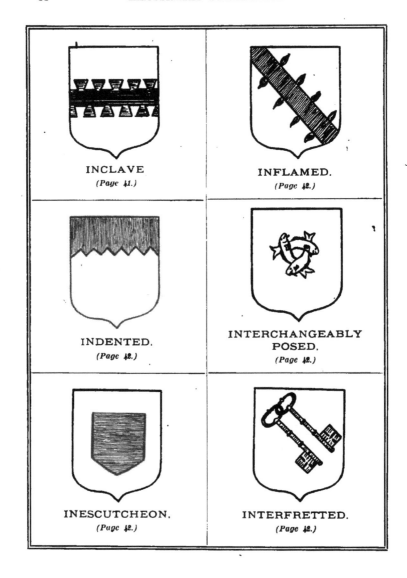

INCLAVE
(Page 41.)

INFLAMED.
(Page 42.)

INDENTED.
(Page 42.)

INTERCHANGEABLY
POSED.
(Page 42.)

INESCUTCHEON.
(Page 42.)

INTERFRETTED.
(Page 42.)

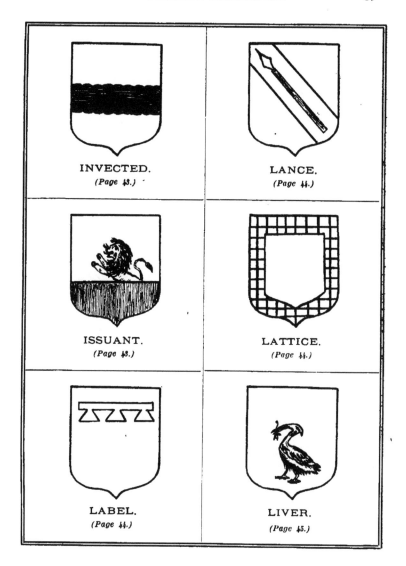

INVECTED.
(Page 43.)

LANCE.
(Page 44.)

ISSUANT.
(Page 43.)

LATTICE.
(Page 44.)

LABEL.
(Page 44.)

LIVER.
(Page 45.)

LODGED.
(Page 45.)

MARTLET.
(Page 46.)

LOZENGY
(Page 45.)

MASCLE
(Page 46.)

LYMPHAD.
(Page 45.)

MAUNCH
(Page 46.)

The above example is from the seal
of John de Hastings (1291).

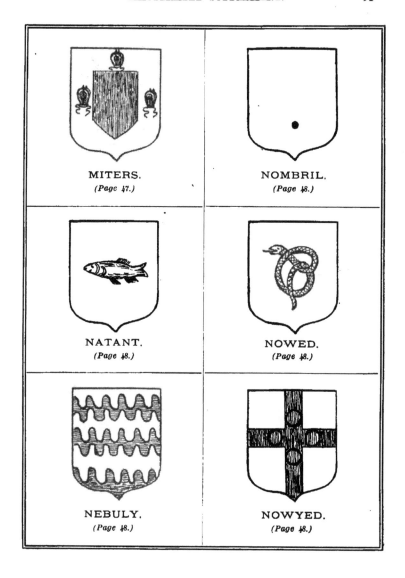

MITERS.
(Page 47.)

NOMBRIL.
(Page 48.)

NATANT.
(Page 48.)

NOWED.
(Page 48.)

NEBULY.
(Page 48.)

NOWYED.
(Page 48.)

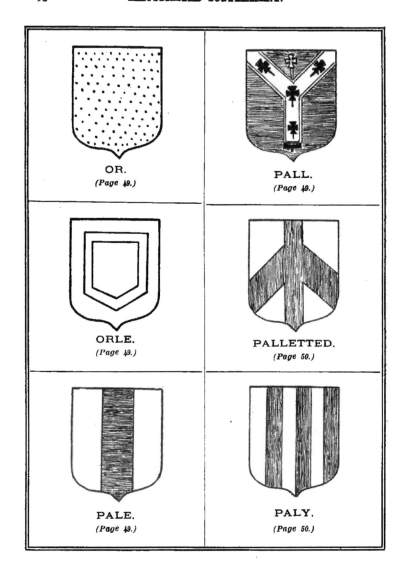

OR.

(Page 49.)

PALL.

(Page 49.)

ORLE.

(Page 49.)

PALLETTED.

(Page 50.)

PALE.

(Page 49.)

PALY.

(Page 50.)

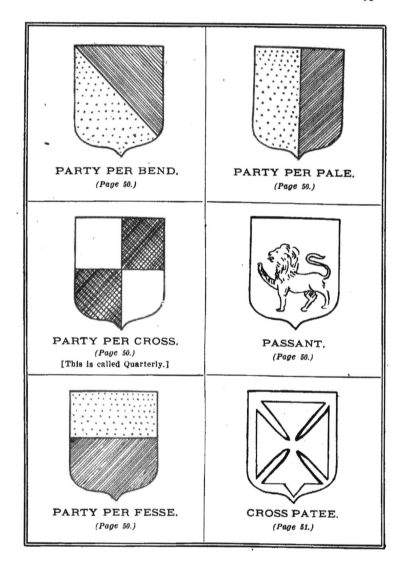

PARTY PER BEND.
(Page 50.)

PARTY PER PALE.
(Page 50.)

PARTY PER CROSS.
(Page 50.)
[This is called Quarterly.]

PASSANT.
(Page 50.)

PARTY PER FESSE.
(Page 50.)

CROSS PATEE.
(Page 51.)

PELICAN IN HER PIETY.
(Page 51.)

POINTS.
(Page 52.)

PHEON.
(Page 51.)

POINT IN POINT.
(Page 52.)

PILE.
(Page 52.)

POMMEE.
(Page 52.)

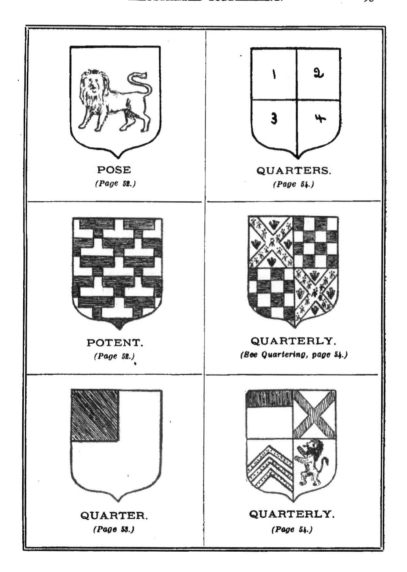

POSE
(Page 52.)

QUARTERS.
(Page 54.)

POTENT.
(Page 52.)

QUARTERLY.
(See Quartering, page 54.)

QUARTER.
(Page 53.)

QUARTERLY.
(Page 54.)

QUARTER-PIERCED.
(Page 54.)

RAMPANT GARDANT.
(Page 55.)

RAGULY.
(Page 54.)

RAMPANT REGARDANT.
(Page 55.)

RAMPANT.
(Page 54.)

RAMPANT SEJANT.
(Page 55.)

RECERCELEE.
(Page 24.)

REST.
(Page 56.)

RECURSANT.
(Page 55.)

ROUNDELS.
(Page 56.)

REGARDANT PASSANT.
(Page 55.)

ROUSANT.
(Page 57.)

SALIANT.
(Page 57.)

SEJANT.
(Page 58.)

SALTIRE.
(Page 57.)

SHAKE FORK.
(Page 58.)

SALTIRES HUMETTEE.
(Page 57.)

SPEAR HEAD.
(Page 59.)

SHIELDS.

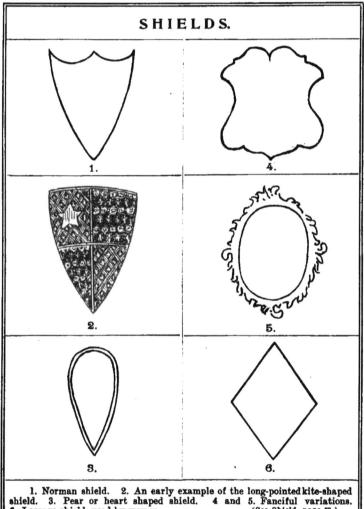

1. Norman shield.   2. An early example of the long-pointed kite-shaped shield.   3. Pear or heart shaped shield.   4 and 5. Fanciful variations. 6. Lozenge shield, used by women.   *(See Shield, page 58.)*

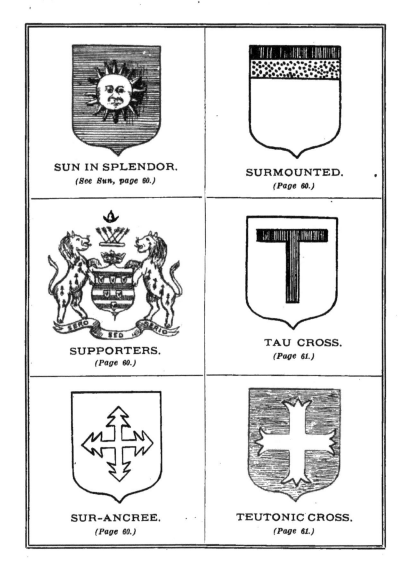

SUN IN SPLENDOR.
(See Sun, page 60.)

SURMOUNTED.
(Page 60.)

SUPPORTERS.
(Page 60.)

TAU CROSS.
(Page 61.)

SUR-ANCREE.
(Page 60.)

TEUTONIC CROSS.
(Page 61.)

TINCTURES.

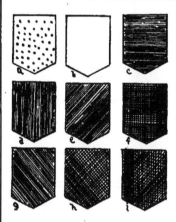

COLORS AND METALS.

a, Or; *b*, Argent; *c*, Azure; *d*. Gules; *e*, Purpure; *f*, Sable; *g*, Vert; *h*, Sanguine; *i*, Tenné.

(For Tinctures see pages 62 and 63.)

FURS.

A, Ermine; B, Vair; C, Ermines; D, Erminois; E, original form of Vair; F, Pean; G, Counter-potent; H, Counter-vair; I, Potent.

THUNDERBOLT.
(Page 62.)

TORQUED.
(Page 63.)

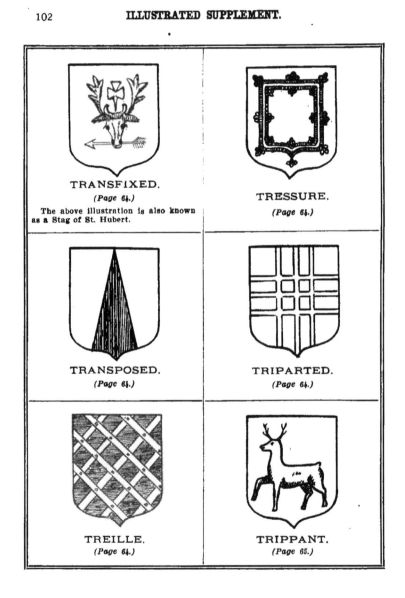

TRANSFIXED.

(Page 64.)

The above illustration is also known as a Stag of St. Hubert.

TRESSURE.

(Page 64.)

TRANSPOSED.

(Page 64.)

TRIPARTED.

(Page 64.)

TREILLE.

(Page 64.)

TRIPPANT.

(Page 65.)

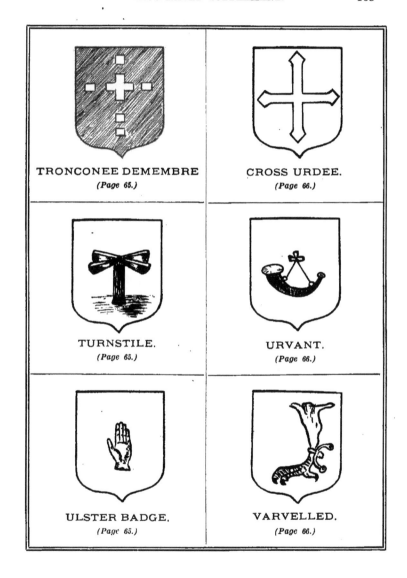

TRONCONEE DEMEMBRE
(Page 65.)

CROSS URDEE.
(Page 66.)

TURNSTILE.
(Page 65.)

URVANT.
(Page 66.)

ULSTER BADGE.
(Page 65.)

VARVELLED.
(Page 66.)

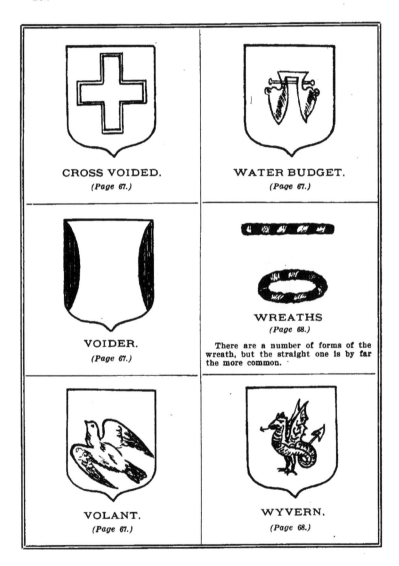

CROSS VOIDED.
(Page 67.)

WATER BUDGET.
(Page 67.)

VOIDER.
(Page 67.)

WREATHS
(Page 68.)

There are a number of forms of the wreath, but the straight one is by far the more common.

VOLANT.
(Page 67.)

WYVERN.
(Page 68.)

DATE DUE

MY 23 70			
MY 3 0'75			
OE 31 '80			

Milton Keynes UK
Ingram Content Group UK Ltd.
UKHW020904220823
427262UK00005B/207